UNSHAKABLE

*Living your life
anchored to
God's Kingdom*

JEFF ROSTOCIL

DESTINY IMAGE® PUBLISHERS, INC.
P.O. Box 310, Shippensburg, PA 17257-0310

"Speaking to the Purposes of God for This Generation and for the Generations to Come."

This book and all other Destiny Image, Revival Press, MercyPlace, Fresh Bread, Destiny Image Fiction, and Treasure House books are available at Christian bookstores and distributors worldwide.

For a U.S. bookstore nearest you, call **1-800-722-6774.**

For more information on foreign distributors, call **717-532-3040.**

Or reach us on the Internet: **www.destinyimage.com**

ISBN 10: 0-7684-3106-9

ISBN 13: 978-0-7684-3106-3

For Worldwide Distribution.

1 2 3 4 5 6 7 8 9 10 11 / 13 12 11 10 09

ACKNOWLEDGMENTS

THANK You, Heavenly Father, for opening Your arms to me and opening my eyes to You. Your Son is the greatest Lover of all time. May my life burn eternally on the altars of Your heart.

I want to especially thank Meljoné, my wife, for your patience and sacrifice while I was writing this book. There were too many late nights and long hours spent writing at your expense. Thank you for loving and serving me beyond the call of duty. You are the delight of my eyes and a remarkable woman of God. I love you.

Thank you to my parents for your unconditional support and encouragement. I love you both.

Thank you, Sean Smith, for your friendship, for believing in me and giving me wings to fly.

Thank you to those who have supported our ministry over the years and helped see this project come to fruition. Your generosity and prayers have helped make this book a reality. Special thanks to Rick, Karen, Mark, Sunny, and Linda for your insights and valuable words of wisdom.

Thanks also to Ronda and the team at Destiny Image for being so cool to work with.

Last, in no way can I take credit for this work. This book is a product of the lives and words of those who have mentored me, both personally and from afar. Thank you. You have blazed the trail that I now tread.

ENDORSEMENTS

Jeff Rostocil is an incredibly gifted teacher and evangelist with a genuine call to the nations. This book illuminates Jesus' favorite subject clearly: the Kingdom of God. It is a must-read for anyone with an evangelistic heart and a willingness to be used by God. It has given me a much deeper level of understanding and insight into the very heart of God and His passion to reach the lost. I now have a greater understanding of the Kingdom of God. My life and my evangelical messages will never be the same. I wholeheartedly endorse this book and pray that it is a huge blessing to you in your ministry as it has been to me. Thank you Jeff and SoleQuest International for the power and purity of your message!

—Steve Wisniewski
Eight-time Pro Bowl guard for the Oakland Raiders

Jeff Rostocil is a gifted communicator whose personal integrity and passionate pursuit of the Kingdom adds substance to his message. This is a book filled with encouragement and challenge for all those who are seeking a deeper understanding of the Kingdom of our glorious King being manifest on earth as it is in Heaven. Read it if you are hungry, read it for greater clarity, and read it if you are interested in a book that will stimulate your faith and motivate your actions.

—Karen Kell
Director of The Healing Rooms, Petaluma, CA

Very few young leaders today have Jeff Rostocil's combination of gifts, character, and visionary leadership. The key idea in this work is Kingdom living. Jeff is equipping people for leadership and imparting a vision of the emerging Kingdom of God. There is no such thing as a formula for effective Kingdom living, but there are foundation principles underlying the growth of such a life. Jeff Rostocil has these principles in place, and he brilliantly shares his secrets in this fascinating book.

—Bruce Glines, executive director
of Serve International
and lead pastor of Sutter Community Church

It has been my privilege to have been associated with Jeff for almost ten years. He was in my church under Sean Smith's tutelage and later on his own as an evangelist. Each experience was marked by an incredible anointing and confirmed with lives being changed. He loves the Word, the presence of God, and his adorable family—a great combo!

My initial thought about another book on the Kingdom of God was, well, not positive but rather skeptical. However, Jeff has captured a whole new aspect and brings it home very clearly. Particularly about contending—it is not automatic nor is it natural; it is free with salvation but must be nurtured. Then to combine that with souls—a natural for Jeff because his real heartbeat is the lost—is excellent. Any topic worthy of discussion needs as many sets of eyes as possible, and Jeff's perspective is very enlightening, insightful, and challenging.

—Bill Bates, senior pastor
Destiny Christian Center, Centralia, WA

And this gospel of the kingdom will be preached in all the world as a witness to all the nations, and then the end will come.

Matthew 24:14

TABLE OF CONTENTS

FOREWORD

I T'S been said that an idea that is not dangerous is not really an idea at all. The church has suffered through seasons where our God-concepts were downsized and our ideas were pedestrian. God's signature move in response is to send a fresh revelation to rescue His Body from falling back into formalism. This revelation is meant to deliver the surrounding community and release a sovereign move of the Spirit. This is crucial, because ordinary solutions will not work with impenetrable obstacles. We should all appreciate that God is not a conventional thinker. When seasons come where there's a fluency of divine ideas, it becomes a prophetic statement of an emerging spiritual architecture and environment.

My great friend Jeff Rostocil has captured one of these dangerous "God ideas" and has put legs on the vital concepts of the Kingdom of God. Some books you read and some books seem to read you—this is one of those readings! As I read this manuscript, I couldn't help but think of how fresh and original this incendiary material is. I found myself drawn in like Moses to the burning bush.

I've known Jeff for close to twenty years and have witnessed his character and conviction. He truly represents a new breed of revivalist that embodies the message and truly lives the hazard with personal sacrifice. Words have always been a powerful army that holds the ability to influence in a way that is undeniably unmistakable, and Jeff is a prophetic, relevant voice releasing a timely message that both empowers and instructs.

This book is a must-read for any who want to be on the forefront of this next move of God. Each chapter builds this Kingdom revelation with the skill of a master craftsman, yet it flows with the rhythm of an artist. You will find yourself alternating between wanting to shout at its fire and wanting to prayerfully contemplate its depth. One thing for sure is that this is not a book that you will read just once. So get ready to take a spiritual adventure that will launch you into greater Kingdom exploits and manifestations. Dangerous times call for dangerous ideas and dangerous deeds!

—Sean Smith,
author of *Prophetic Evangelism*

INTRODUCTION

D ARKNESS is daunted by the thought of another great awakening. Great awakenings have always catalyzed great advances in the Kingdom of God, but before there can be a great awakening there must first be a rude awakening. The western church is in the midst of a rude awakening.

We are realizing that mass-marketing schemes and church growth gimmicks do not broaden the Kingdom of God nor fulfill the Great Commission. We are discovering that dead programs and denominationalism are often nothing more than feeble attempts to fit God into our agendas. We have painfully learned that celebrity ministers, opulent cathedrals, professional worship services, and hype may more quench the spirit of revival than promote it.

The church has always been God's primary means of extending His Kingdom, but without His presence we have grown barren and anemic. But we are not without hope. Our current state is not our ultimate fate. Heaven is blowing a resounding trumpet, and God is awakening us to the reality of a present power. We will once again be a mighty voice to the nations.

This awakening is not only touching our churches but our nation as well, for a sentiment of political disdain is brewing in the cauldron of our culture. A generation is growing increasingly dissatisfied with how government operates while at the same time becoming more demanding of it. Americans are not just losing faith in the political process; we are losing faith in our ability to govern ourselves.

Man has always sought new ways to govern people. While monarchies, aristocracies, democracies, and republics all have great strengths, they are also plagued with grave weaknesses. History has proven that each has done the world much good and caused the world much grief. In the wake of this grief is a society left disillusioned by all that is institutional and organized, including religion.

But there is a government that has been established over the earth since the dawn of time. It was birthed long ago in the heart of God. It is like no other. It is a heavenly Kingdom.

This righteous administration is not controlled by politics, special interests, or power struggles. It is a holy regime and a uniting kingdom, a sovereign and universal empire. Its economy is unlimited, and its leader is infinite.

Since the conception of the world, the Lord has been preparing a Kingdom for His people and a people for His Kingdom (see Matt. 25:34). He is marshalling a company of Kingdom-minded revolutionaries, and I believe you are one of them. I invite you to explore the wonders of this Kingdom with me as we carry the torch to a lost world.

I do not consider myself an authority on the Kingdom of God. There are many others who have taught and lived the Kingdom far better than I. But if these modest thoughts are not profound, I trust they are practical, for they are revolutionizing me. My prayer is that they revolutionize you.

CHAPTER 1

UNSHAKABLE

"We are receiving a kingdom which cannot be shaken."
(Hebrews 12:28)

IT was October 17, 1989. I was a freshman at San Jose State University when the Loma Prieta earthquake rocked the Greater Bay Area. The 7.1 magnitude quake collapsed freeway structures, damaged countless buildings, claimed dozens of lives, and left more than 12,000 people homeless.[1] The shaking lasted less than 20 seconds, yet it was enough to trigger a tsunami off the coast of Monterey and halt game three of the World Series at Candlestick Park for ten days.[2] The tremor sparked a total of 27 fires across the city of San Francisco,[3] leaving an estimated $10 billion worth of damage.[4] Who can forget when one section of the Bay Bridge suddenly gave way, crushing several cars underneath?

I remember an eerie silence settling in over the Silicon Valley after the earthquake struck. I lived with my parents in the South Bay Area not far from the epicenter, and our house shook like an episode of *Soul Train*. My mother's glass hutch crumpled, shattering all of her china. Our big-screen television landed on top of the dangling VCR, ruining the screen. In my room, books, clothes, trophies, frames, and lamps decided to play scrum, and I found them stacked in a pile on the floor like linemen scrambling for a loose ball. Throughout our neighborhood, several chimneys collapsed and two houses had to be evacuated and condemned.

Three years prior to the earthquake, my father purchased property in the hills of Los Altos and employed the help of my brother and me to build a house. This was the house I came home to that day. As we surveyed the damage to our home, amazingly the foundation was unmoved and the walls remained structurally sound. My father had wisely built upon solid rock.

The Crazy Glue of Life

The world in which we live is shaky—cars break down, stock markets crash, marriages fall apart, athletes get injured, politicians break their promises, and heroes disappoint. If that is not enough, life as we know it is precarious. We are only allotted a few determined revolutions around the sun before our trophy accomplishments and earthly possessions end up in a pile on the floor. The attrition of life eventually wears down our frame, and what we thought was unbreakable was in fact terribly unstable. Like a toppled chimney, we all eventually grow up, grow old, and are grown over.

But the human spirit is interminable and longs to build something that outlives itself: a company, a career, a dynasty, a technology, a medical breakthrough, or a timeless work of art. Man won't be satisfied with a black box that melts or a wristwatch that stops ticking. King Solomon explained why, saying that God has *"set eternity in the hearts of men"* (Eccles. 3:11 NIV).

Our Inventor has placed deep within us a longing for prominence that can never be satisfied without a quest for permanence. Whenever God sets something in motion, it rolls timelessly, and no earthly function can arrest it. In other words, the Kingdom of God is eternal, and only that which is eternal can awaken our hearts. Society is madly searching for something unshakable to invest in. The world is unknowingly looking for a kingdom, and only in the Kingdom of God will their souls find the stability they crave.

The Kingdom of Heaven

The Kingdom of God awakens every poem the human heart longs to pen. It is the politician's greatest dream, the scientist's chief conclusion, and the painter's crowning masterpiece. It trumps every philosophy, every society, and every religion known to humankind. To the spiritual vanguard it is the ultimate expedition, the final frontier of the unseen world. Every agency, activity, institution, and organization on earth is humanity's attempt to find God and His reigning presence on earth.

Martin Luther King, Jr., caught a glimpse of this beautiful Kingdom. Quoting the prophets Isaiah and Amos, he prophesied about the Kingdom of God while preaching on the steps of the Lincoln Memorial, saying:

> I have a dream today! I have a dream that one day on the red hills of Georgia the sons of former slaves and the sons of former slave owners will be able to sit down together at the table of brotherhood. I have a dream that my four little children will one day live in a nation where they will not be judged by the color of their skin but by the content of their character. I have a dream that one day right there in Alabama little black boys and black girls will be able to join hands with little white boys and white girls as sisters and brothers. I have a dream that one day every valley shall be exalted, and every hill and mountain shall be made low, the rough places will be made plain, and the crooked places will be made straight; "and the glory of the Lord shall be revealed and all flesh shall see it together."[5]

The dream he dreamt and the nation he envisioned encompassed more than just a free society or a liberated America. He saw a heavenly Kingdom and died a martyr for its cause.

God's ruling commonwealth is the emancipation proclamation of our souls. It is a divine declaration of humanity's independence from the clutches of tyranny and the cruelty of oppression. We are familiar with the regimes of the earth that have brought forth change and liberty, but we are largely ignorant of the enterprise of Heaven that has come to free our souls. While the kingdoms of this earth may have accomplished noble things, the Kingdom of Heaven is the only one to have conquered the great divide—the gap between God in Heaven and humanity on earth.

The Great Domain

A kingdom is traditionally defined as a region that is subject to the reign of a king. It is a jurisdiction over which the influence of a king has full authority.[6] The Greek word for kingdom is *basileia,* which means "royal power, dominion, and the right to rule."[7] This indicates that a king's realm is not only a territory but a dominion. Simply put, a kingdom is a king's domain.

Basileia comes from the root word *basis* which means "foot or walking."[8] The implication here is that every place a king walks is his jurisdiction and his domain. So we could easily say that the jurisdiction of the Kingdom of God is wherever the King treads His foot. Where the King manifests His presence, there His reign is firmly established. Where He exerts His authority, there is His sovereignty.

In addition, kings are historically the reigning lords of the land. A lord is not only the property owner but also the overseer. Spiritually speaking, the King of Heaven is the Lord and Owner of the planet we live, work, and play on. We are God's property, and the appointed manager of the real estate called earth is Jesus Christ. The Kingdom comes to us when we acknowledge Him as our Lord.

God's Elevator

The phrases *the Kingdom of Heaven* and *the Kingdom of God* are found almost ninety times in the gospels and well over a hundred times in the New Testament. They are used interchangeably as synonyms. *Kingdom of Heaven* is exclusive to the book of Matthew and is referenced nowhere else in the Bible. There is little, if any, distinction made between the two in Scripture.

Scripture indicates that the Kingdom of Heaven is God's universal intention for the earth (see Matt. 6:10, Rev. 11:15). Think of it is an invisible world that blankets the visible. It is not confined to this galaxy, much less a building, a church, or a brilliant mind. Its headquarters are not found in a palace or a temple but in Heaven. It belongs to Heaven and originates in Heaven.

Heaven in Greek is the word *ouranos* and can be translated "the universe."[9] This demonstrates that the Kingdom of Heaven is more than an earthly kingdom; it is a universal one. It is far superior to any authority on earth, for it has a greater jurisdiction—the entire universe. Just as the earth is subject to the laws of the universe, so the governments of the earth are subject to the Kingdom of the universe. Every president, prime minister, and dictator technically rules under the jurisdiction of the King of Heaven. Christ is truly the King of *all* kings.

Ouranos is also rendered "an elevated sky," revealing that this heavenly Kingdom always elevates.[10] It elevates people out of obscurity, nations out of poverty, cultures out of depravity, and souls into prosperity. People thrive when the Kingdom of God arrives, for it introduces a higher way to live—a life governed by the Most High.

Heaven is a Kingdom

Heaven not only has a Kingdom, but the pattern of Heaven *is* a Kingdom. The highlight reel of Heaven captures more than Peter guarding the pearly gates or people dancing on streets of gold. The highest ecstasy of the afterlife is not playing a harp with angel friends on cloud nine in a continual state of bliss. The glory of Heaven is found in the throne room. This is where all of the action takes place. This is *the* place to be for eternity.

Heaven would not be a paradise without the presence of God, and all things were created from, revolve around, and will end before His sovereignty (see Rev. 22:1). The most honorable seats in Heaven are those closest to the Infinite One, and the "Who's Who" of eternity can be found among that company.

To stand in the presence of a king is a great honor, but to stand before the King of kings is the greatest honor afforded any being. When Elijah stood before King Ahab, he proclaimed, *"As the Lord God of Israel lives,* **before whom I stand,** *there shall not be dew nor rain these years, except at my word"* (1 Kings 17:1). Elijah was not intimidated to stand before an earthly king because his life was lived standing before a heavenly One. Leonard Ravenhill once said, "A man who is intimate with God will never be intimidated by men." When we live our lives before God, we will not be afraid to live our lives before men.

The Seven Angels

And I saw the seven angels who stand before God, and to them were given seven trumpets (Revelation 8:2).

The book of Revelation is an action-packed sneak peek at the emerging Kingdom of Heaven. John reveals that seven angels stand around God's throne day and night. They are not jealous of Gabriel's job assignment, nor do they wish to be fighting some spiritual battle with Michael. They are not somewhere lost in the celestial Kingdom sweeping glory dust off the streets of gold. They stand before God continually. They have been afforded one of the greatest joys possible—to be in close proximity to the King. Scripture foretells that these nameless angels will one day sound a revolutionary trumpet that makes end-time history.

Like these angels, you and I are beckoned to stand continually before God's throne, ready for assignment. Though we may be nameless and faceless to the kings of this world, we have full access to God's throne. We have no need to envy another person's call, because we have been afforded the greatest honor. If the King wants to trumpet a message on earth, may we be close enough to be handed a horn. And if He never hands us an assignment, at least our lives are only better for being lived in the presence of God.

Life in the Kingdom is a life lived before God's throne. His throne room is our courtroom and our refuge. When we become aware that the eyes of God are always upon us, we tend to live better and wiser. We are bolder in our witness, gentler with our tongues, more patient with our children, more tender with our spouses, more respectful of our parents, more diligent with our time, more obedient to traffic laws, more mindful of our thought life, and more selective of what entertains us.

Indestructible

The Kingdom of Heaven is truly out of this world. The curiosity that our culture has with UFOs and aliens is merely an inner cry for something from another world to invade ours. The Kingdom of Heaven is the fulfillment of that cry. It is a heavenly invasion coming literally from another world. The lost city is not Atlantis or some ancient civilization. It is the City of God. To taste and see it is to taste and see something divine.

Over three thousand years ago, King Nebuchadnezzar dreamt of a stone that struck the kingdoms of the world. This stone soon became a great mountain that stood forever and influenced the whole earth. Daniel interpreted this to mean that God is going to establish an everlasting Kingdom that will never be destroyed and will eclipse all other kingdoms on earth (see Dan. 2).

As ambassadors of Christ, our announcement to this world is that there is a foundation for living that is unseen and indestructible. Like my father's house, our Heavenly Father is constructing a mansion for His family built upon an Eternal Rock. It will be the greatest house ever built. It is not a house of cards but a house of diehards, for its inhabitants take on its resilient nature. Even when disaster strikes trials will not destroy them, for life in this household eliminates all that is destructive—destructive behavior, destructive relationships, and destructive thinking.

Conclusion

There has never been a more appealing and dominant force on earth than the reigning presence of Heaven. A life built upon this foundation stands as a monument for generations to come. When all else goes down, it rises. When all is lost, it is triumphant. When everything is shifting, it is unshakable.

This magnificent Kingdom is approaching. Make way for the King. God's economy is coming to shake every kingdom that is in rebellion to Heaven; but before it shakes the world, it wants to rock yours. You can either choose to fall upon the Rock now and be broken, or you will be crushed when it all comes crashing down. Regardless, we will all be shaken. But while the world is quaking, Heaven's King will emerge glorious and victorious.

Endnotes

1. BBC, "1989: Earthquake hits San Francisco," *On This Day*, http://news.bbc.co.uk/onthisday/hi/dates/stories/october/17/ newsid_2491000/2491211.stm (accessed March 26, 2009).

2. Kenji Satake and Hiroo Kanamori, "The origin of the tsunami excited by the 1989 Loma Prieta earthquake," *Geophysical Research Letters* 18, no. 4 (April 1991), http://adsabs.harvard.edu/ abs/1991GeoRL..18..637S (accessed March 26, 2009).

3. "San Francisco Earthquake History 1915-1989," Museum of the City of San Francisco, http://www.sfmuseum.org/alm/quakes3. html (accessed March 26, 2009).

4. Dan Goldstein, "Earthquake Museum: 1989 Loma Prieta Earthquake," OlympusNet: First Internet Service Provider for the Olympic Peninsula, http://www.olympus.net/personal/gofamily/ quake/famous/prieta.html (accessed March 26, 2009).

5. Martin Luther King, Jr., "I Have a Dream" (speech, Lincoln Memorial, Washington, D.C., August 28, 1963).

6. Myles Monroe, *Rediscovering The Kingdom* (Shippensburg, PA: Destiny Image, 2004), 125.

7. Joseph Thayer, *The Online Bible Thayer's Greek Lexicon* (Ontario, Canada: Woodside Bible Fellowship, 1993).

8. James Strong, *BibleSoft's New Exhaustive Strong's Numbers and Concordance with Expanded Greek-Hebrew Dictionary* (Nashville, TN: Thomas Nelson Inc., 1994).

9. Joseph Thayer, *The Online Bible Thayer's Greek Lexicon* (Ontario, Canada: Woodside Bible Fellowship, 1993).

10. James Strong, *BibleSoft's New Exhaustive Strong's Numbers and Concordance with Expanded Greek-Hebrew Dictionary* (Nashville, TN: Thomas Nelson Inc., 1994).

THE MESSAGE OF THE KINGDOM

"...the kingdom of God has been preached, and everyone is pressing into it"
(Luke 16:16).

The message of the Kingdom has never been more relevant than today. As stewards of a fallen planet, it is imperative that we grow in our understanding of the Kingdom and how to communicate its message. Aristotle wrote, "It's not enough to know what we ought to say. We must also say it as we ought." In other words, what we preach is equally as important as how we preach it. These next few chapters are designed to stockpile your spiritual arsenals with Kingdom truths and equip you to boldly communicate with power the Kingdom of Heaven.

CHAPTER 2

THE GOSPEL OF THE KINGDOM

*"After John was put in prison, Jesus came to Galilee,
preaching the gospel of the kingdom of God"* (Mark 1:14).

THE first chapter of Mark was Jesus' coming-out party. It records that His popularity spread throughout the region after He came out of the desert victorious and full of power. He taught a fresh yet ancient doctrine in the synagogues.

The abbreviated edition of His first sermon is found in Matthew: *"Repent, for the kingdom of Heaven is at hand"* (Matt. 4:17). Mark, however, gives us the unedited version: *"The time is fulfilled, and the kingdom of God is at hand. Repent, and believe in the gospel"* (Mark 1:15).

According to the gospel of Mark, Jesus' first public statement baptizes the world with the knowledge of the Kingdom. It was not just a message from Heaven; it was *the* message.

Jesus went about all Galilee, teaching in their synagogues, preaching the gospel of the kingdom, and healing all kinds of sickness and all kinds of disease among the people (Matt. 4:23).

...He went through every city and village, preaching and bringing the glad tidings of the kingdom of God (Luke 8:1).

...I must preach the kingdom of God to the other cities also, because for this purpose I have been sent (Luke 4:43).

Jesus' Favorite Subject

Jesus fully embodied the message of the Kingdom. He spoke publicly of the Kingdom for over three years, teaching truths, telling stories, giving analogies, instructing His disciples, feeding hungry crowds, and demonstrating with power the Kingdom of Heaven. The spotlight of almost every parable He told was the Kingdom, and even after His resurrection He is found tutoring His disciples about the Kingdom of God (see Acts 1:3). The Kingdom seems to be His favorite subject.

This initial discourse of the Messiah indicated His principal purpose for coming and set the stage for the rest of His ministry. He did *not* begin by teaching about hell, the antichrist, or loving your neighbor. Although He would eventually address these matters, He had a more judicious declaration to make. He proclaimed the gospel of the Kingdom.

The Rescue

There is a difference between the gospel of the Kingdom and the gospel of salvation. They express the same gospel but emphasize different truths.

The gospel of salvation is the element of the good news that liberates us from original sin. It protects us from eternal judgment and restores our relationship with God the Father through the finished work of Christ. This gospel teaches we are baptized into the death, burial, and resurrection of Jesus and given the Holy Spirit as a down payment for our redemption. We are now saved by grace through faith, and it requires a hearing ear, a believing heart, and a profession of faith to appropriate it. These glorious truths have the power to deliver us from our crimes against God and their consequences (see Eph. 1:13 NIV).

The message of salvation is not really about the afterlife, and we cheapen the good news when we make it only about Heaven and hell. Making it to Heaven was clearly not the central focus of Christ and the early church, nor should it be ours. The apostles never dangled the luxuries of Heaven over people to motivate them to respond. While forgiveness and grace are foundational themes running through God's redemptive story, salvation alone is not the entire gospel. There is also the gospel of the Kingdom.

The Ruling

The gospel of the Kingdom builds upon the truths of salvation and enriches our understanding of them. If salvation is *the rescue of humanity* by God, then the Kingdom is *the ruling of humanity* by God. It is more concerned with motives and actions than with creeds and confessions. Salvation is the means by which we gain access to God's favor and eternal life, but through the Kingdom we cultivate faithfulness and maturity, because it deals directly with the allegiance and government of our hearts.

When I was 18 years old, Jesus was Savior of my life but not Lord. Though I had made a decision for Christ at the age of 5, I was not yet a disciple. Sports, girls, and popularity consumed the passions of my heart.

That all changed in a moment's notice when an injury to my knee set off a chain of events that only God could orchestrate. My girlfriend and I were in the midst of a break-up. Not only did the nature of the injury limit my athletic ability, but it also forced me to drop out of my first semester of college. All that I was pursuing was suddenly kicked out from under me.

Lying in the hospital, alone and afraid, the Lord visited me. He asked for my heart, calling me out of compromise and into His Kingdom. Christ would not share me with the world. He wanted all of me or none of me. In tears, I surrendered. That proved to be the best cry of my life.

I call that night my adult conversion, when my faith truly began to blossom. While I was familiar with what it meant to be rescued by Christ, I wasn't familiar with being ruled by Him. It was now time, however, to turn my creeds into deeds, and it was this encounter that sparked the genesis of my journey into the Kingdom.

The Kingdom of Heaven is the inheritance of our salvation and the responsibility of the saved. It is why we are saved and paints a more complete picture of who Jesus is. If honoring Jesus as *Savior* is the offspring of salvation, then honoring Jesus as *Lord* is the offspring of the Kingdom. Our conversion frees us from the grip of the world, but the Kingdom arms us to infiltrate a sinful world and have influence in God's world.

Jesus preached the gospel of the Kingdom above salvation because salvation is found within the Kingdom. When we emphasize the new birth to the exclusion of the Kingdom, we inadvertently make justification our high-water mark, neglecting those things that bring us into maturity, like repentance, obedience, prayer, lordship, discipleship, community, and loving one another. Both the gospel of salvation and the gospel of the Kingdom are invaluable to the good news. But in order to come to a place of prominence in God, we must move beyond the truths of redemption and operate in the realm of the Kingdom.

Progressive and Emerging

The gospel of the Kingdom emphasizes that Christ is physically coming to rule the earth. Like an emperor entering a city, His coming will be celebrated, and like a general invading a province, His army will be dreadful. He will right all wrongs, and we will write new songs. He will overthrow the wicked, install a one-world government, and rule the planet with the saints of God (see Rev. 5:9-10). This holy new world order is called the *coming* Kingdom of God.

But the Kingdom of Heaven is not just rapidly approaching; it is currently among us, and a dimension of the Kingdom has already come. It is both emerging *and* existing. The Bible speaks of a present kingdom age and a future kingdom age (*Present:* Matt. 21:28-32, Mark 9:1, Luke 11:20, 19:11-27, 22:29, Col. 1:13; *Future:* Ps. 72:7-8, Dan. 2:44-45, 7:14,27, Matt. 26:29, Luke 13:28-29, 19:11, 21:31, 22:18, 1 Cor. 15:22-26). Both are revolutions that restore the rule of God. The *coming* Kingdom is revolutionary and will bring a radical shift to the way the earth is governed. It will be ushered in with the return of Christ. The *current* kingdom is also revolutionary and brings a radical shift in the way the human heart is governed. This is the age we now occupy.

The Kingdom comes first to reign in our minds, homes, and communities before it ever seeks to reign on earth. God is establishing an *internal* rule in us first before His *eternal* rule has gone public. The battle for the earth is no different than the battle for our hearts. It is about who controls the landscape. When a heart has but one king and a people choose to be ruled solely by the Lord, the Kingdom freely takes root there.

An un-ruled heart lives in anarchy toward God, and in order for God's Kingdom to surge God-rule must replace self-rule and every other ruler. This is the *current* Kingdom of Heaven, and the closer we get to the coming Kingdom the more we will see the current Kingdom sculpting God's people from the inside out.

I am told the title "lord" was traditionally reserved for those valiant enough to prove themselves on the battlefield.[1] If this is true, then we serve a valiant King. Moses describes Him as a "Man of war," and David calls Him *"the Lord mighty in battle"* (see Exod. 15:3; Ps. 24:8). God not only fights our battles for us but also with us, and as His children we possess His gladiator spirit. We are a warrior race, born for battle, destined to fight. One day we will rule *with* Him, but only to the extent we allow ourselves to be ruled *by* Him.

During the week of my 30th birthday, the Holy Spirit informed me that the next decade of my life would be more about family than about ministry. Up until then I had remained single, giving my twenties to the Lord and ministry. His words were not what I expected to hear, but looking back they were indeed prophetic, for the decade of my thirties brought to me a wife, children, and a home.

Starting a family later in life has its advantages and challenges, and one of those challenges for me was embracing flexibility. Unknowingly, I had become rigid before I married Meljoné. I was accustomed to spending my time and money as I pleased, but all that would need to change if I wanted a successful marriage and family.

In the same way, the call to the Kingdom challenges our flexibility. We can no longer live as we have been living. We can no longer spend or do as we always have, nor do we want to. Our newfound commitment to the Kingdom becomes a spiritual renovation that produces a reformation of the soul. Because the Kingdom is progressive and is still progressing, it requires that we embrace change in order to keep in step with its rhythms. Our service to the Kingdom of Christ then becomes a perpetual movement toward change and expansion.

This remarkable form of personal government is surprisingly obtainable. Operating out of this progressive-Kingdom mentality helps us mature into confident leaders, more patient spouses, respectful children, loving fathers and stronger mothers. As we become transformed by Christ, every area that we are designed to influence burgeons. Life in the Kingdom then becomes a beautiful and tangible expression of what happens when Christ is given complete allegiance.

The Future of the Earth

This gospel of the Kingdom will be preached in all the world as a witness to all the nations, and then the end will come (Matthew 24:14).

Notice that Christ says the gospel of the Kingdom will be preached as a witness to the nations, not the gospel of salvation. I am not trying to split hairs between the two, but the reason why the message of the Kingdom must be proclaimed is because every people group must prepare to accept the return and reign of Heaven's King. The announcement and invitation of the Kingdom prepares the way for Christ to enter in and leaves the nations without excuse on Judgment Day.

Scripture indicates that the Lamb of God will not only come back to rule the earth for a millennium, but God the Father will also make His habitation on the earth. Heaven is coming down here. In fact, one day there will be a new Heaven, a new earth, and a New Jerusalem where the Heavenly Father will dwell with humankind forever. The saints will be His people, and He will be their God, and this will all take place on the third rock from the sun (see Rev. 21:1-3).

This is the reason why we are not instantly transported to Heaven upon conversion. The mission of Christ is not to get us up there, but to create an atmosphere down here that He can inhabit. *"...When the Son of Man comes, will He really find faith on the earth?"* (Luke 18:8). God is seeking a society on earth that replicates Heaven.

The Even-ing News

Gospel means *good news,* but sometimes we are guilty of reducing the gospel to just wishful thinking. We plead: "Accept Christ! He will save you from your troubles, and you will go to Heaven." What an embarrassment! This is a grave misrepresentation of the good news of Jesus Christ.

What makes the good news so good is that it is relevant, timely, urgent, and liberating. The message of the gospel is not that God's people will become so defeated by the surrounding evils of the world around them that God will one day have to steal them away to an eternal bomb shelter. Our idea of the second coming is erroneous if we expect the Lord to beam us up from this God-forsaken world to live like monastic Christian escapists in the sky.

The good news is that there is restoration available for those who currently reside on the earth. When believed, the gospel assures with hope that our broken lives can be invaded by the goodness of God on this side of eternity. George Ladd writes, "The Kingdom of Heaven belongs to the future, and yet the blessings of the Kingdom of God have entered into the present age to deliver men from bondage."[2] The gospel was never tailored just for the afterlife then and there, but for your current life here and now.

When my daughter was born, she spent the first seven weeks of her life in the hospital. She was ten weeks premature and weighed just over two pounds at birth. Her torso was about the length of a credit card, and I have pictures of her body fitting in the palm of my hand.

In the midst of that trial, however, my wife and I were never without peace. God's transcending presence sustained us. What concerned the doctors did not concern us, for we knew that goodness will prevail in the end. (See Romans 8:28.) Only the gospel can bring this kind of assurance.

I am pleased to report that Soraya today is a joyful and intelligent 3-year-old with no health issues to speak of. The place of our greatest test has become the place of our greatest testimony. Our litmus is now our witness. Like Job, God graciously restored with interest all that was lost, and now that chapter of our lives is one of our most triumphant.

Victory in the Midst of Snakes

I am not advocating that the Kingdom life is utopian, nor am I am implying that those who enter the Kingdom will never face hardship. The Kingdom of God is not Fantasy Island. Acts 14:22 says, "*We must through many tribulations enter the kingdom of God.*" The truth is that Christ's followers may have more tribulations because of who we are and Whose we are. If they persecuted our King, what will they do to us?

When the good news truly penetrates every facet of our being, however, the final chapter of our lives will not end bitterly. Our life stories are not fairy tales, and this is precisely why we need Heaven to invade our shattered lives. People don't need to know how to escape their problems; they need to know how to live victoriously through them. The issue is not so much our fumbles, failures, or financial woes, but rather our tenacity about placing Christ in the center of our crisis. The Lord chose not to take away the serpents from the Israelites when Moses prayed, because He wanted them to have victory in the midst of snakes. This is the Kingdom of God.

To the addict living on the streets of Amsterdam the gospel is not that if he recites a form prayer he will one day be in Heaven. This is not the good news and only serves as a low and unrealistic motivation for change. The good news for him is that he does not have to live another day in darkness, being dependent on a drug for his happiness. He was created for a high purpose—the higher life!

We need to equip him to stand up to his giants, not accept them. We need to offer him freedom from his demons, not counsel them out of him. We need to give him the power to drive away his depression, not tell him how to cope with it. People should not be comforted in their dysfunction or made to feel better about their cowardice. They are dying to know how to confront and conquer the enemies of their soul. Politics can't do it. Education won't do it. The gospel is the only solution.

Conclusion

Every revolution begins with a revelation, and this revolution is fueled by a revelation of a King with a message. Christ not only spoke of the Kingdom; He is the Kingdom, and just as He is more than a Savior, the gospel is more than salvation. His principal mission on earth was far bigger than our eternal security; it was to please His Father. As the Kingdom begins to dominate our thinking, we come to realize that life less about us and more about our Father.

Christ's mission has now become our message, and this message is the gospel of the Kingdom. I admit there may never be a more challenging time to boldly stand for the gospel of truth than today, yet there may never be a time more necessary. Be strong and courageous.

Endnotes

1. Kingsley Fletcher, *I Have Seen the Kingdom* (Orlando, FL: Creation House, 1998), 27.

2. George Eldon Ladd, *The Gospel of the Kingdom* (Grand Rapids, MI: Eerdmans Publishing Co., 1959), 140.

CHAPTER 3

GETTING BEYOND YOUR SELF

"It is a great sign of true repentance when a man approves of the justice of his own punishment." —Hugo Grotius

I loved watching sports growing up, and before ESPN there was ABC's *Wide World of Sports*. Every Sunday afternoon I would count the hours until it aired. The beginning of the program was truly magnetic. It opened with clips of great athletic achievement set to inspiring music with the golden voice of Jim McKay saying, "Spanning the globe to bring you the constant variety of sport; the thrill of victory and the agony of defeat."

All who watched the show will never forget the devastating highlight of a ski jumper who topples end over end off the side of the jump, ripping through a fence and smashing violently into a snowy embankment. For my generation, this epitomized the agony of defeat.

I was always curious who this infamous ski jumper was and what kinds of injuries he sustained. After some research, I discovered his name is Vinko Bogataj from Slovenia. The crash took place at the 1970 World Ski Flying Championships in Oberstdorf, West Germany. Amazingly, Vinko walked away with only a slight concussion, but what is more surprising is that he had no intention of completing the jump.

On that fateful day, a snow flurry blanketed the mountain as the event began. It was Vinko's third jump. By this time the conditions on the ramp had worsened, and ice became a threatening factor for the jumpers. As Vinko shot out of the starting gate, he felt that the ramp had become too slick and too fast. He feared he would land well beyond the safe sloping area, putting himself and others in danger. So, he tucked to slow himself, but in the process he lost his balance and slid off the ramp. That one decision etched his name in modern athletic history.

There is a spiritual application that can be drawn here. Sometimes we get halfway down the ramp of a decision only to realize that we have taken the wrong course of action. Unknowingly, we have put ourselves and others in danger. We are faced with a crucial decision to either carry on as usual or change. To redirect one's course in life can sometimes be a dramatic and painful undertaking, but change is always better than a fatal landing at the end.[1]

I believe people can change. I believe cities can change. I believe the alcoholic and the pedophile can change. I believe you can change. I believe I can change. I would not be writing this book if I believed otherwise. If people cannot change, we are all doomed to living fatalistic lives, and our hopes of Christ-likeness are dashed.

...Repent, for the kingdom of Heaven is at hand (Matthew 3:1-2).

God believes people can change, but not without His help. When Jesus and John hiked out of the same desert preaching the same message of repentance, it was no coincidence. They were calling humanity out of spiritual desolation and into Kingdom consolation, out of the agony of defeat and into the thrill of victory.

Thieves and Prostitutes Welcome

Repentance requires humility, which is always our first step toward the Kingdom. The gospels reveal that prostitutes and thieves were entering the Kingdom ahead of the religious experts simply because they had humbled themselves and heeded John's baptism (see Matt. 21:31-32; Luke 7:29-30). They caught a revelation of Jesus and were among the first to recognize Him as Messiah when He arrived on the scene. Their willingness to repent opened their eyes to reality.

Those who refused to humble themselves and submit to John's baptism overlooked what they were looking for. Tragically, they missed their day of visitation and discarded the very answer to their prayers. Pride blindfolded them from seeing Jesus from Heaven's vantage. These are those *"whose minds the god of this age has blinded, who do not believe, lest the light of the gospel of the glory of Christ, who is the image of God, should shine on them"* (2 Cor. 4:4).

As we will discover, repentance is not a bad word. In fact, it is a liberating word and has a beautiful side to it. It paves the way for a visitation of Christ. When applied, it removes the veil that obstructs the carnal mind from receiving Kingdom truth and grants the penitent eyes to clearly see the King.

Repentance Redefined

What comes to your mind when you hear the word repent? I get images of the angry evangelist pointing his boney finger right through my soul, or the bearded street preacher holding a placard that reads, "Repent, ye, for the end of the world draweth nigh." Thankfully, the message of repentance is more practical and radical than these images.

Since we are called to preach repentance, let's define it. Repentance is not godly sorrow, the conviction of sin, having a guilty conscience, or making an apology to God. While it may include all of these elements, repentance still goes further. Repentance is when we acknowledge our sinful activity and stop doing what grieves the heart of God. Repentance is confessing and forsaking sin. It is the action of it, not the emotion. *"He who covers his sins will not prosper, but whoever confesses and forsakes them will have mercy"* (Prov. 28:13). Confessing is what we say; forsaking is what we do. And repentance requires both.

A Sunday school teacher once asked her class of second graders what repentance means. A boy promptly raised his hand and said, "It is being sorry for your sins." The teacher thanked him for his response. A little girl then raised her hand, and said, "It is being sorry enough to quit." The little girl got it right.

The Smell of Satan

When I was a boy we lived on several acres of land just east of San Jose, California. Every year there was a particular eucalyptus tree that was home to a bird's nest. One spring day I scaled the tree, peeked inside the nest, and found three un-hatched eggs. Not knowing any better, I picked them up, examined them, and carefully placed them back inside the nest.

After climbing down, I patiently waited to see mama bird come flying home to care for her soon-to-be chicks, but she never returned. She deserted the nest. My scent caused her to utterly forsake her precious eggs, abandon her family, and start over in another tree.

In the same way, repentance is not just an admission of wrongdoing. It calls for abandoning the action altogether. Repentance leads us to forsake the nest of our ways, pleading with us to never again return to that tree. However precious or profitable the sinful behavior may seem, it has the smell of satan all over it. We should take flight immediately and build an untainted nest in God's branches. The person who continually returns to their old ways only allows eggs of death to hatch and mature in their nest (see James 1:15).

The Process of Repentance

Repent is a military term meaning to turn around. The Jews used *shuwb* to define repentance, which means "to restore or return to the starting point."[2] The Greeks employed *metanoeo*, which is "a total reconsideration or change of mind."[3] When people repent, they reconsider what they thought to be true and reorganize their world according to

God's standard of truth. This paradigm shift completely alters one's God-view, world-view, and self-view. It involves the will of the mind, because one must think to turn around before one can ever actually turn around. *Metanoeo* is the conscious decision to turn around and have a true change of heart.

Repentance is like a spiritual weed killer. It effectively tills the soil of the heart so that the seed of God's word can fall on good ground and produce a fruitful harvest. It is God's refining process and will ultimately bring congruency between flesh and spirit. By eliminating the polarity between our human nature and our heavenly nature, the spirit is then freed to resonate with God's Spirit. When our flesh has the same yes and amen as our spirit does, we know we have fully repented.

Repentance is both a decision and a practice. As we have repented, so we continue to repent, for the call to repentance is as much for the believer as it is for the lost.

This became painfully clear when the Lord showed me how much fear I still hid in my heart. As a boy, I had fears, and those fears seemed to grow old with me. I'm not afraid of the boogieman anymore, but I do still battle the fear of failure, rejection, and appearing foolish.

For me, fear and discouragement are like drinking buddies. The more I give into fear, the more discouragement plagues me, and they both are working to accomplish the same goal—to separate me from my courage. Discouragement always follows a decision to delay action, and any trace of discouragement in my heart is usually the result of undefeated fear in my life.

Fear is more than just an emotion or a spirit—it stands in opposition to God's nature (see Matt. 10:28, 25:25, 2 Tim. 1:7, 1 John 4:18). I am not speaking here of godly fear, but the kind that fears people above fearing God. Fear that is sinful is simply faith in the wrong kingdom, and I have had to come to realize that every time I obey anxiety or worry I am dis-obeying God.

As Kingdom communicators, we must submit to the process of repentance first for ourselves. We cannot articulate what we refuse to demonstrate. A wise person sometimes changes his or her mind, but a fool never does. And if we cannot change our minds, we cannot change anything.

Cotton Candy Kingdom

One shade of *metanoeo* reads, "The ability to get beyond self," which suggests that the message of repentance has the capacity to do what nothing else can—untether you from you. It liberates us from the dictation of self and unlocks our hidden potential in Christ. It is life lived at a higher plane and at a higher octane. We are now empowered to get ourselves over, because we have been empowered to get over our selves.

The last time I had cotton candy, I resolved to never do it again. Not because of the taste but because of the disappointment. What looks like a tantalizing treat ends up merely being a measly tablespoon of sugar.

Self-gratification is like cotton candy—elusive and unfulfilling. It puffs itself up, appearing colorfully delicious, but lacks real substance. Self tries to convince us that we can please ourselves by helping ourselves, but is there anything more monstrously ugly than self-absorption? The biggest lie of the planet is that when I finally get what I want I will be happy. The world sings, "Look out for number one," but don't believe the propaganda. Inner satisfaction comes only when we seek to please another, and being wrapped up in ourselves makes for a pretty small package.

Thankfully, God's Kingdom can deliver us from the need and desire to please ourselves. For the lover of God, repentance is not a chore but a cheer. We don't repent because we have to but because we want to, knowing that it pleases our Lover. If you are serious about plunging into Kingdom exploits, think seriously about canceling your membership to the club of self. You cannot expect to enter God's Kingdom without leaving your own, and we only dupe ourselves when we assume we can walk in our own kingdom and still inherit God's.

Kingdom Policies

The chief duty of every foreign diplomat is to carry out the policies of the nation they represent, regardless of personal opinion. Since we are ambassadors of Heaven, we must carry out the policies of the Kingdom we represent and live the way Heaven desires regardless of how we see things. My personal opinion about lying does not matter. If I feel that a white lie is acceptable behavior, I must reform my feelings about lying to match the will of the administration I represent, as well my behavior. If my King says fornication, gossip, and resentment are unacceptable, I must repent if I think and act otherwise.

> *There is a way that seems right to a man, but its end is the way of death* (Proverbs 14:12; 16:25).

Some preach that there are two paths in life. One path leads to God, while the other path leads to destruction. This may be true, but really there is just one spiritual path that leads to life or to death. It just matters which way we are traveling on it.

Jesus and John were calling for a radical change of direction. They beckoned, "Your life is traveling in the wrong direction. Turn around! The Kingdom of Heaven is the opposite way." This is repentance. It is not just a sermon. It is an invitation to encounter the King of the universe.

New School Camping

Camping has come a long way, and I recently learned that there are two kinds of camping. There is old-school camping, and there is new-school camping.

Old-school camping is what I grew up with. It is roughing it. You find a forest, pitch a tent, draw water from the stream, fish for dinner, cook meals over an open fire, hang your food in a tree, sleep in a sleeping bag, and always have a gun handy. This kind of camping is peaceful and respects the land. It is memorable and educating.

New-school camping is radically different. It is luxury camping. You pull up your RV in the reserved slip and attach sewer lines and electricity. You have a gourmet kitchen complete with oven, microwave, and granite counters. Hot showers and a latté await you in the morning and saunas and king-sized beds at night. Oh, and don't forget the stainless-steel barbeque on the porch and the high definition plasma with satellite hookup hanging on the wall. With new-school camping, you don't have to get dirty or even have to go outside to camp. It's basically your living room on wheels.

Some people have been told that they can follow Christ without repenting of their old lifestyle. This is like new-school camping. It is basically their old life on wheels. They go to church, sing songs, repeat prayers, and drop a few bucks into the plate. They are in a new place, new surroundings with new friends but are the same old person on the inside. Their language, attitude, values, thoughts, and money management remain unchanged.

Repentance demands both a turning *to* and turning *from*. In order to turn toward something, one must first turn away from something else. Both are required. To fully enter the Kingdom, a person must fully turn his or her back to sin, and to the extent that he or she repents is the extent he or she seizes the Kingdom of God.

The action of turning *to* is equally as important as the turning away, for a person cannot successfully turn away from something without simultaneously turning toward something stronger. This is called the explosive power of a fresh affection. Without it, change is only provisional. This explains why addicts cannot find freedom through willpower alone. An addict may temporarily arrest the urge, but if he or she has nothing stronger to turn toward, the addictive lifestyle will eventually return. Praise God that the law of the Spirit is more powerful than the law of sin and death (see Rom. 8:2). Christ is our one-step program.

Right actions always follow right thinking. If right actions do not follow a profession of faith, neither they nor we have begun the process of repentance. A person who claims to love God but continues his or her lifestyle of sin is still, by definition, an unrepentant sinner.

Comfort Without Cost

My wife and I once ministered to a man on the brink of a nervous breakdown. His life was in shambles. His business ventures were failing. He had just been released from a drug rehabilitation center, and after a bitter breakup with a long-term homosexual partner, he was deeply depressed. We found him lonely, hopeless, and suicidal.

We reached out to him with the good news, and he acknowledged a need for God in his life. He was ready to say "the prayer" but was unwilling to proceed when we explained that it would require change. He had no conviction of sin and no intentions of altering his behavior. Being homosexual was his identity, and he felt God was requiring too much of him by asking him to change his lifestyle.

Traditionally, we would have overlooked this mammoth detail and led him in a prayer anyway, presuming he would eventually work it out along the way. But this time we did not. Our friend was clearly not ready to follow Christ. He refused to be willing to change what needed to be changed. He was interested in the benefits of the cross without bearing the sacrifice of it. He wanted the comfort of Christ without the cost. Although he knew his behavior was destructive, he rebuffed the only path that could lead him to a liberated heart.

Jesus made it clear that there is a cost to discipleship, and following Christ for this man was just too costly. Although we did pray with him and for him, we did not lead him to believe that his lifestyle was pleasing to God.

I encourage you to use caution before you lead someone in a verbal decision that his or her heart is unwilling to make. Commitment without conviction can open a person up to unnecessary condemnation, disappointment, and failure, and it can also be counterproductive to the work of salvation in his or her life. Charles Finney was known to forbid people from converting to Christ until there was clear evidence a full measure of conviction had run its course in their hearts. Maybe this accounts for the estimated 80 percent of his converts staying true to Christ.[4]

Apostolic Preaching

The power of conviction was highlighted once to me in a dream that shook me to the core. I was walking along a path through a college campus and suddenly around the corner appeared a giant of a man. He stood tall, majestic, and fierce. His eyes were intense, and he looked like a prophet right out of Scripture. I said to my walking buddies, "Who is that mighty man of God?"

Immediately, he marched straight toward me and singled me out. His countenance was severe, and I was intimidated. As he approached, I backed away from him and stumbled to the ground. Lying flat on my back and looking straight up at him, I watched as he pulled an axe from his clothes and dropped it into my chest. I felt my soul reverberate, and I woke up trembling.

As I pondered the vision, the Holy Spirit revealed to me that the man was the angel of conviction and that the axe represented the preached word. I believe the Lord is releasing a greater authority in this day to preach the Word with prophetic conviction. He is singling out a generation of fierce warriors whose tongues have been sharpened by the Word and whose words are pregnant with conviction. Like Paul, their preaching will either stir revival or start a riot.

> *The Kingdom of God is not in word but in power* (1 Corinthians 4:20).

Jonathan Edwards knew this power. Knox, Wishart, Wesley, Whitefield, Brainerd, and Finney all knew this power. What they saw was mighty in their day. It shook the world and caused great awakenings. It toppled mighty people and mighty empires, but this next move of God will far surpass theirs. Imagine a whole company of believers walking in a greater purity, passion, and power than these mighty revivalists! This is what the Kingdom of God will look like as we approach the end of this age.

The Kingdom cannot move forward without a clarion call to repentance. On the day of Pentecost, Peter preached with unusual certainty as he called the multitudes to repent. Luke records that the people were cut to the heart and 3,000 were converted (see Acts 2:37-42).

Kingdom preaching is "cut to the heart" preaching. It releases a spirit of conviction on our words and our witness. Like Jesus and John, you and I are Kingdom revolutionaries supplied with a baptism of repentance. John Steinbeck put it this way: "One person with their mind made up can shove a lot of people around."

The Stigma

You will likely not win any popularity contests preaching repentance both inside the church and out. There is a stigma attached to it, but maybe the reason why we are so soft is because we have tried to get by without it. Instead of repentance we have preached a watered-down, "Barney" version of the gospel and settled for comfortable and convenient conversions. Perhaps we have placed too much stock in the installment plan of salvation. We've preached grace, hoping sinners would eventually change their ways and be nice to God. Unfortunately, they sometimes never come to appreciate the full measure of God's forgiveness, because they never truly understood they were sinners in need of forgiveness. To them, the cross becomes largely meaningless.

I have found that trying to bring people into the Kingdom without repentance is like trying to hit a homerun without a bat. It is frustrating and futile. Many do eventually modify their behavior, but many more find themselves defeated, deceived, and under the impression that they have entered the Kingdom of Heaven. Over time they become finicky, flaky, and easily offended. They eventually grow bitter at God and disgusted with the church and seek peace through ulterior means.

On the other hand, preaching repentance does not give us license to be jerks. Being critical, crass, or unnecessarily offensive is not of the Spirit of God. Our job is to invite them in, not drive them away. Truth can either heal or destroy; it just depends on the mouth and the motive. Some preach hell like they want people to go there. This is not the heart of Heaven. We are to preach the truth in love (see Eph. 4:15), and if I have no love in my heart for people, I have no right to preach truth to them. Without love, it should be spiritually illegal to preach truth. *"Though I speak with the tongues of men and of angels, but have not love, I have become sounding brass or a clanging cymbal"* (1 Cor. 13:1).

"Ain't No Valley Low Enough"

The desert that Jesus and John came out of is known as the Jordan Valley. It is the lowest elevation on earth at 417 meters below sea level (1,369 feet).[5] I recently visited this valley. It is east of Jericho, where the mouth of the Jordan River prepares to spill into the Dead Sea. This is also the area where Elijah was believed to be caught up into Heaven in a whirlwind.

This prophesies to us. Jesus and John went to the depths of the earth in the spirit of Elijah to preach a message found in the depths of God's heart. Through repentance, God takes people to the very core of their being, revealing their lowest and ugliest parts. As they respond to God's recipe for change, they become spiritual ski jumpers, elevated to a high place and gaining altitude in God's domain.

Sometimes God will take people to the depths of a valley to show them that He will never leave them so that when He takes them to the heights of Heaven He knows that they will never leave Him. Repentance is that journey. It can turn a dead sea and a dry desert into an oasis of glory. When obeyed, the lowly and the humble are lifted heavenward as Elijah was.

...the goodness of God leads you to repentance (Romans 2:4).

Conclusion

Because the Kingdom of Heaven is more spiritual than political, it can only be gained through a spiritual response. Repentance is that response. Jesus said that Heaven throws a party when one sinner repents, which means repentance is not just for a human's happiness, but also for God's (see Luke 15:10). Teaching a person to repent of his or her ways is one of the greatest ways you can serve him or her, and it is God's passion that compels us to speak up.

Don't hesitate to bring your hearers to repentance. Be bold. Take up the mantle of Elijah and go forth in the spirit of Jesus. If we refuse to preach repentance, we are doing an eternal disservice to those seeking to enter the Kingdom of God.

Endnotes

1. Craig Brian Larsen, *Illustrations for Preaching and Teaching* (Grand Rapids, MI: Baker Books, 1993), 21; http://espn.go.com/abcsports/wwos/milestones/1970s.html, accessed April 25, 2009.

2. Francis Brown, S. Driver, and C. Briggs, *BibleSoft's Brown, Driver and Briggs' Hebrew Lexicon* (Ontario, Canada: Woodside Bible Fellowship, 1993).

3. James Strong, *BibleSoft's New Exhaustive Strong's Numbers and Concordance with Expanded Greek-Hebrew Dictionary* (Nashville, TN: Thomas Nelson Inc., 1994); Joseph Thayer, *The Online Bible Thayer's Greek Lexicon* (Ontario, Canada: Woodside Bible Fellowship, 1993).

4. Winkie Pratney, *Revival* (Springdale, PA: Whitaker House, 1983), 123.

5. Janet Larsen, "April 7, 2005: Disappearing Lakes, Shrinking Seas," The Earth Policy Institute, http://www.earth-policy.org/Updates/2005/Update47_data.htm (accessed March 27, 2009).

CHAPTER 4

HUMAN RITES

"I'm losing my religion." —Michael Stipe of R.E.M.

S OMETIMES the best way to define something is to define what it isn't. While the Kingdom of God is spiritual, it is not religious.

Worldly religion is like the tower of Babel. It is humanity's pious attempt to climb up to God through works and enlightenment. It is soulish and often not spiritual. It employs the fruitless deeds of the flesh in an effort to manufacture that which can only be produced by the Spirit of God. While most religions advertise spirituality, they lack the most essential ingredient—the Spirit. The Bride of Frankenstein and religion have two things in common—they both are man-made and ugly!

Fear-driven religion is terribly evil. It manipulates people's sense of guilt and uses familial loyalties to imprison families for generations. It aims to keep people so preoccupied with religious activity that they are too busy to hear truth and too bound to accept it. Religion usually has good intentions but lacks the power to live it out. Unfortunately, terrorism, bigotry, hatred, and war have all employed the religious to trumpet its agenda, and historically more crimes have been committed in the name of religion than we like to admit.

Abandoning Christianity

Most outsiders view Christianity as just another world religion. Our churches are listed in the religious section of the yellow pages. Our books are cataloged with religious interest books in bookstores. This is not their fault but ours. Our track record indicts us. Historically, we have acted very much like a religion instead of a Kingdom.

The greatest black mark against those who profess Christ is our own behavior. We have our own rituals, liturgy, lingo, titles, ceremonies, denominations, church clothes, Christian flags, and golden crosses. No wonder unbelievers view those who follow Christ as religious when they see the way Christ is represented.

A religious spirit has successfully conned its way into the community of Christ. This hierarchical system squashes the laity and accuses all who challenge it of being rebellious. It holds the most capital and has the loudest mouths in the church but does very little to advance the Kingdom. Religion is what we are rescuing people from, not calling them to, and it is out of this religious system that we must exit before we can expect the world to follow.

We often argue that Christianity is not a religion but a relationship. This is true, but the highly unbiblical terms "Christendom" and "Christianity" smell of religion to most people. Who gave us these phrases anyway? It is not Scripture, and it certainly was not God. It is the world.

The term "Christian" originated with unbelievers (see Acts 11:16; 26:28-29). Peter is the only biblical apostle to use this phrase to describe a believer, and the only other New Testament writer to say a positive word about religion is James (see 1 Pet. 4:16; James 1:26-27). Jesus clearly did not come to establish a new world religion, and the Bible never speaks of a Christian religion. Rather, the New Testament promotes a pure and undefiled community that includes caring for widows and orphans.

> *Pure and undefiled religion before God and the Father is this: to visit orphans and widows in their trouble, and to keep oneself unspotted from the world* (James 1:27).

Of course, true Christianity is a relationship. Followers of Christ do indeed have relationship with the Father through Jesus Christ, but it might be better said that Christianity is not a religion but a kingdom. It might be even be better to abandon the word "Christianity" altogether.

I have stopped calling myself a Christian and using the term Christianity to define my faith. It is not that I dislike these terms, but I dislike what they have come to represent in our culture. Many call themselves Christian but are not truly seeking Christ-likeness. In order to make a distinction, I prefer the phrase "believer, follower, or disciple of Christ." I believe these speak less of organized religion and are more accurate in representing true relationship. More important than the sub-title, however, is the substance. If we are going to use the word Christian, let's start living like one. Then we can work on the terminology.

As Old as Cain and Abel

Religion and the Kingdom of God are as opposite as Cain and Abel. Cain offered a sacrifice of works while Abel offered a sacrifice of faith. Cain brought an offering of dead fruit; Abel brought a living sacrifice. Cain spilled juice; Abel shed blood.

> *By faith Abel offered to God a more excellent sacrifice than Cain* (Hebrews 11:4).

God refused Cain's offering because he never bothered to ask God what kind of offering He desired. Religion does the same. It seeks to worship God in its own manner, ignoring what God desires or requires. While religion may attempt to *appease* God, it can never *please* Him. The best that religion can offer is a bloodless sacrifice of self-effort.

When God covered Adam and Eve's shame by supplying them with animal skins for clothing, He performed the first animal sacrifice. It must have been heart-wrenching for them to witness an innocent life slaughtered right before their eyes for their rebellion. The death of a perfectly good animal served as a deterrent for sin even under the old covenant and established a precedent for ages to come. Cain thought that some really nice fruit would atone for his sins, but we know now that only innocent blood can. Religion has the tendency to underestimate the power of sin, just as Cain did.

Around the World in 35 Days

I once had an encounter with religion that I will never forget. It was the summer of 1997, and at the time I was serving as a campus pastor at Chico State University in Northern California. I was a part of two overseas outreach teams bound for North Africa and Southeast Asia. My older brother was working as a missionary in Belgium, so I decided to stop by to visit him on my way to Africa.

After touring Europe for a few days, I spent two intense weeks of ministry in Africa and another two weeks leading a team in Thailand. It was a fruitful summer, and in the process I fulfilled a boyhood dream. Starting from California, my flight plan flew eastward around the globe.[1]

As I spent considerable time on three continents representing three major world religions, I was astonished to observe how similarly they all worshipped. Each religion had idols, statues, temples, male priests, holy water, burning candles, consecrated garments, modesty rules for women, and sacred pilgrimage sites. What was baffling was that these three dominant world religions could not possibly be more diametrically opposed to one another in beliefs. They celebrated opposing gods and conflicting doctrines; they fought holy wars and slaughtered one other; they wore different hats and distinctive costumes, but to me they all seemed to dance to the same religious tune. It was their resemblance, not their disparity, that shocked me.

On our final day in Thailand, we toured a Buddhist Temple. It was our free day—our time to rest, buy souvenirs, and sightsee. After walking up an enormous flight of stairs, we were escorted into a large courtyard behind a locked gate. Here, the priests and monks performed their duties. We could not wear trousers, so they gave us garments to put over our clothes, and we had to remove our shoes. Along the way I spotted this gigantic gong. Without hesitation, I grabbed the mallet and let out a resounding noise. This would prove to be a regrettable decision, because I didn't realize this gong was used to conjure up spirits. Oops.

That evening, I suffered from the worst headache I have ever had. It was so intense that I collapsed in my hotel room after barely dragging myself through the lobby. I fell asleep in my clothes and woke up 24 hours later, dazed and drenched with sweat. It was a miracle I made it to the airport on time for my flight home.

From that day forward, my spiritual sensitivity went dormant. Passion seemed missing and the voice of the Lord was strangely silent. When it finally dawned on me that my participation at the temple constituted as idol worship, I confessed it, but it took almost a year and half to get free from the curse of that incident. Hard as that may be for some to believe, it was even harder to endure.

I quickly learned that religion is more than a system or an institution; it is a spirit, and this spirit is powerfully effective. It attempts to dull a person's spiritual senses and squeeze the life out their faith. Religion acts very much like a vaccine. It injects people with a near-dead, inert version of the real so that when the actual comes along they reject it. Religion can so familiarize someone with the things of God that they remain inoculated to a true visitation from Heaven. The result is that people actually become spiritually immune to revival.

This spirit is also subtle. Like an intelligent disease, it has the ability to mutate to survive. It can sit in the front row of our finest churches faithfully every Sunday, pay tithes, lift hands, shout "Amen!" and still not be cast out. To our discredit, it has been given a place among our ranks. I am convinced that nothing has robbed us more of experiencing the grace of God than religion has, and unfortunately most of us live with some form of it.

> ...the chief priests held a consultation with the elders and scribes and the whole council; and they **bound** Jesus, **led** Him away, and **delivered** Him to Pilate (Mark 15:1).

It was a religious spirit that led the chief priests to bind and deliver the Son of God to Pilate. When allowed to rule, this spirit can render

Christ powerless in our lives, short-circuit our prophetic promises, and lead us to crucify the very answer to our prayers. Whereas the spirit of religion restricts people and keeps them bound through compulsion, the Spirit of the Kingdom liberates people and binds them together through citizenship.

Handmade, homemade religion attempts to work its way to Heaven, but the opposite is true with the Kingdom. It originates in Heaven and has been forcefully advancing on earth. The aspirations of religion are to get *us to Heaven* through performance, but the objective of the Kingdom is to get *Heaven to us*. Jesus exposed the lie of religion and He forever removed the handcuffs of those straight-jacketed by the demands of a religious system. Only in Him is the spirit of religion defeated.

The Way of Cain

Cain went out from the presence of the Lord and dwelt in the land of Nod...(Genesis 4:16).

Woe to them! For they have gone in the way of Cain...(Jude 11).

The way of Cain never leads to the presence of God. Cain left God's presence and became a fugitive. He was exiled to a land east of Eden called Nod, which means *wandering* (see Gen. 4:9-16).

What distinguishes the Kingdom of God from religion is the presence of God. Visit the Dome of the Rock or the Church of the Holy Sepulcher in Jerusalem, and it becomes evident that religion is what is leftover once God leaves. The world wants all the privileges of God's presence without the prerequisites, and this is the trap of religion.

As Kingdom brokers, we traffic in the presence of God. The religious are starved for the peace of Heaven and the voice of God, and our job is to expose them to these realities. Like the woman at the well, when they taste of this water, not only will they come running but they will also bring the village people with them!

Making Eye Contact With God

When I was in college, the Holy Spirit became my music instructor and taught me how to play the piano. I would sit for hours at the baby grand in my parent's living room longing just to play one song for the Lord and remorseful that I didn't stick with lessons as a kid. So, I asked the Holy Spirit to teach me, and He did! What is more, He also taught me the guitar and drums. He truly is a gifted Teacher.

For several years, I led worship for our church and for various gatherings, but I struggled with really enjoying it. I felt so inadequate leading others in worship, partly because I didn't know what true worship was. All too often the music got in the way. I would be so focused on leading the band or playing the right note that I would forget to point my being vertical.

Still, at times, the music gets in the way for me. For a season, I could not listen to a worship CD without being distracted. Worship songs became more of a hindrance than a help, because I felt shackled to the words of the song. I could only go where they were taking me, and my spirit wanted to go somewhere else. Silence became my instrument of worship, because with silence the spiritual avenues are unlimited.

It is not that there is anything wrong with our worship songs or worship meetings. It's just that we cannot always rely on them to take us to the throne room. We must allow the Holy Spirit to be our worship leader and our spirits to follow.

I am discovering that worship is so much more than music. It is a heart that makes continual eye contact with God. It is more internal than external, less about body posture and more about heart posture. Worship is when our spirit engages God's Spirit. The goal of worship is not merely to express myself to God. It is to find the face of God.

> God is spirit, and those who worship Him must worship in spirit and truth (John 4:24).

The way of Cain leads us away from true worship and the presence of God. Truth without the Spirit results in dead works and passionless faith. Likewise, spirituality without truth leads to spiritism, emotionalism, and false doctrine. It is imperative that we contend for both spirit and truth in our worship. This means we should instruct people to worship God in the way He prescribes, not in their own way.

Characteristics of a Religious Spirit

Being religious is not a compliment. Athens was the religious capital of the world in Paul's time, yet it was the most ignorant of the Kingdom of God (see Acts 17:16-24). What concerns me, though, is not so much the work of religion in the world but the work of religion among us. A religious Christian is far more threatening to the Kingdom than any world religion.

Can you identify a spirit of religion when it is in operation? Here are some characteristics:

- Spiritually haughty
- Unteachable
- Finicky
- Not open to correction
- Claims to take orders directly and only from God
- Seeks to be recognized for piety
- Passes judgment on others
- Unnecessarily strict on others and self
- Quick to point fingers
- Sees the wrong more than the right
- Feels called to correct everyone and everything
- Critical of new movements and unorthodox expressions of faith in Christ
- Is either hyper-emotional or repulsed by over-emotionalism
- Devotion to God is more mechanical than relational

- Actions motivated more by duty than by love

- Appeases God through good deeds, church attendance, Bible knowledge, and prayer

- Tend to bargain with God

- Sees and calls other things religious

- Deep down a religious person feels terribly insecure, knowing that he or she will never measure up to his or her own standards, much less God's. (Parts taken from a sermon by my pastor, Napoleon Kaufman, in 2003.)

A religious attitude can be easy to spot in others but strangely difficult to observe in ourselves. Let the Holy Spirit search you. If you find any of these qualities in your own heart, as I do at times, renounce these ways and come out of alignment with a religious spirit. It may take a lifetime to shed our religious clothing, but the hope of being clothed with Christ is far worth it.

Replacing Form With Flame

How does one come out of religion and into the Kingdom? Through the fire of God. Because religion is a *form of godliness* that denies the power of God, ridding ourselves of it requires abandoning the *form* to embrace the *flame*. We have to let go of our liturgy to embrace the liberty of Christ. What would happen if we discarded our orders of service and our predetermined song selections? What if we stopped boasting about our apostolic call and started calling ourselves bondservants of Christ? What if we spent the offering collections on building people instead of a new building? What if we stopped our canned approach to evangelism and sought to be led by the Spirit in our witness? We might readily rely more on the Holy Spirit and in the process discover that we need each other. We might actually see the Kingdom of God come with power.

The community of believers my wife and I are a part of is not your traditional church. We do not own a building or have preset orders of service. We don't pass out bulletins or have song solos during offering. We meet in our homes, eat together, pray together, read the Word together, ask questions, discuss Scripture, celebrate the feasts, prophesy, pray for the sick, and minister to one another. It is not a home group or a Bible study. It is our church.

At first, we felt guilty not attending a traditional Sunday morning church service. We have never known anything different. Yet, this leading was not sparked by hurt or rebellion in any way. In fact, more the opposite is true. It has been our longing for genuine fellowship with fellow believers that has led us on this surprising journey. We found it far too easy to be plastic in large group settings, so we decided to become intentional about refusing to settle for inauthentic relationships.

The Kingdom call insists that we press into relationship, authenticity, and accountability, not escape from it. Through this process, Meljoné and I have stumbled upon a vibrant, life-giving community of believers, and we find ourselves more committed to loving the people of God than ever before. In order to receive new wine, however, we had to abandon an old wineskin. The form could not contain or sustain the new flame He had for us.

> *...Cain who was of the wicked one and murdered his brother...* *because his works were evil and his brother's righteous* (1 John 3:12).

The sibling rivalry between Cain (which means *spear*) and Abel (which means *breath*) continues today. The religious system of Cain is still working to deal a death blow to the Kingdom of God. Nothing can halt a move of God faster than religiosity, and if given a voice it will eventually snuff out the breath of God in our congregations.

To defeat religion in our own lives, we must refuse to wear the mask of sanctimony. This means we must contend for the presence of God in our worship gatherings, in our witness, and in our homes. This does not mean we throw out all tradition. Godly tradition is rich and healthy as long as it doesn't lay aside the commandment of God (see Mark 7:8-13). Sometimes in our quest to become nontraditional we have actually become more religious. But as we come out of religion, undoubtedly our expression of

Christ will change, and hopefully we will paint a more accurate portrait of Christ to the world we are aiming to reach.

Conclusion

The Kingdom of God doesn't have a pretentious religious bone in its body. It is a movement without organizational walls. There are plenty of religions in the world to choose from, and Jesus did not see the need for another one. He saw the need for a Kingdom.

Both Heaven and the heathen are turned off by dead religion, and as co-laborers with Christ, we neutralize the gospel when we make it into a professional institution. Do we really believe that hiring professional musicians to lead our worship will cause the devil to retreat? Is another church growth seminar really necessary? Would Jesus sanction emotional manipulation to drum up large offerings? I can assure you that a new program or a new building is not the answer for you and your community. The answer is right under our noses—each other.

Christ commissioned us to promote the Kingdom, not capitalism. Refuse to allow the political arena, the media, or the morals of Hollywood to hijack your expression of the Kingdom. Ask the Holy Spirit to help all of us see the difference between Heaven's culture and western culture.

And preach the Word. What the world needs to hear is Christ—crucified, risen, and coming again. Only when we grow intolerant to the spirit of religion in our own lives will we be able to defeat it in and through our message to the world.

Endnote

1. In Africa, we smuggled and distributed Arabic Bibles past the watchful eyes of border patrol. Because we were ministering in a strict Muslim country, we had to rely on the guidance of the Holy Spirit for our evangelism efforts. The Lord was faithful to set up divine appointments for us every day, and several Muslims came to know Christ in the process. In Thailand, our team preached Christ

and prayed for many sick children. Over five hundred children proclaimed Jesus as their Lord through various public school outreaches arranged by the local elders.

CHAPTER 5

THIS PRESENT FUTURE

"In the same way that Jesus is fully God and fully man,
so the Kingdom is fully now and fully then."
—Bill Johnson[1]

THERE are two advents of the Kingdom—an initial phase and a consummate phase. One is partial. One is perfect. One is coming. One has come. But the question remains, "How much of the Kingdom of God has already come?"

The herald and forerunner of the Kingdom was John the Baptist. He is one of the greatest Kingdom preachers the world has ever seen. Jesus called John more than a prophet, saying he was the Elijah to come. He is depicted as a burning, flaming torch, clothed in camel hair, eating locusts and honey.

I once read that a visit from a king must be prepared for in advance and that when a king arrives he must be properly announced. John did just that. This uncivilized man was the trumpeter, awakening men's hearts to the Kingdom and illuminating the way for the earth to receive its King. And like most revolutionaries, he was beheaded for it.

Greater Than John

For I say to you, among those born of women there is not a greater prophet than John the Baptist; but he who is least in the kingdom of God is greater than he (Luke 7:28).

Some teach that the Kingdom of God is only a future glory; that it has yet to arrive and is not currently active on earth. But if this were true, in what way are the least of us greater than John? Will you and I truly be greater than John in the Kingdom to come?

Jesus was not insulting this great prophet. He was talking about the current advent of the Kingdom, not the one yet to come. Between John's death and our new birth something significant happened—the Kingdom arrived. John could only see the Kingdom from a distance because the work of regeneration was not yet complete, but now we are privileged to receive something that even the greatest prophet never received—the seal of the Holy Spirit. John's ceiling became our floor. Jesus opened the Kingdom door to all who knock when He ascended to the right hand of God, and now the least of us have access to a realm that even John did not.

Age of the Spirit

This present dispensation can be characterized as the age and work of the Holy Spirit. The Holy Spirit does in us what Christ has done for us. He is the spiritual expression of the physical work of Christ. He is presently achieving in us the victories Christ has won for us.

The Spirit of God and the Kingdom of God are not synonymous but not mutually exclusive either. The Spirit of Truth has come to help advance the Kingdom of God through us, and He has taken up residence in us so that we can take up residence in God's Kingdom. He is a foretaste of the life approaching. Where the Spirit is given liberty to operate, the Kingdom flourishes, and the level that we yield to Him is the level that the Kingdom manifests.

Jesus remarked to a group of skeptics, *"If I cast out demons by the Spirit of God, surely the kingdom of God has come upon you"* (Matt. 12:28). *Has come* means to *have arrived.* So, with the advent of the Holy Spirit came the release of the Kingdom, even among the unbelieving.

The Main Event

Jesus also said, *"Assuredly, I say to you that there are some standing here who will not taste death till they see the kingdom of God present with power"* (Mark 9:1). Jesus performed many signs and wonders through His ministry, but John did not. (See John 10:41.) What Jesus promised, John only saw from afar. Why? Could it be that you and I have been brought into another spiritual arena that John the Baptist wasn't—the Kingdom of God *present with power?*

I've always assumed that the death and resurrection of Jesus was the main event of the New Testament, and that the coming of the Holy Spirit was a secondary work of Christ. We tend to view the sacrifice for sin and His victory over death as the primary mission of the Messiah, and the sending of the Holy Spirit was an added bonus of that achievement. But what if the opposite were true? What if the main assignment of Christ was to pass the baton on to the Holy Spirit, and that Jesus' death and resurrection were the necessary events making it possible for us to receive the Holy Spirit? Is it possible that the crowning work of Christ is the marrying of the Holy Spirit with the human spirit so that we could rule the nations with equity in the emerging Kingdom of God?

The Hungriest Man Alive

John G. Lake is one of my heroes in the faith. Known as a man without compromise, he was described as the hungriest man for God alive. His life and ministry saw many profound miracles both in America and on foreign soil.

Lake was born in Ontario, Canada, in 1870 and was one of sixteen children. He was converted to Christ at the age of sixteen.[2] He notes that his childhood was filled with memories of "sickness, doctors, nurses, hospitals, hearses, funerals, graveyards, and tombstones." He writes that "for 32 years some member of the family was an invalid" and that "during this time our home was never without the shadow of sickness."[3] Soon, eight of his fifteen siblings had died of disease.

When John was a boy, he suffered from rheumatism in his legs. He was brought to John Alexander Dowie's healing home in Chicago, and during prayer his legs instantly straightened out. This one miracle turned Lake's world right side up, for it planted in him a powerful seed of truth, a truth the world desperately needed. But like any truth, it had to be tested in order to grow stronger.

The Day That Changed Everything

The test came when another one of his sisters fell deathly ill. Out of simple faith and sheer desperation, he contacted Dowie in Chicago, and the two fervently prayed for her healing. After a long spiritual battle she was completely healed, and God birthed a healing ministry in John's heart. This one event catapulted him into a lifelong mission to destroy the works of the devil.

During Lake's lifetime, he oversaw several churches and planted hundreds more in South Africa and the United States. He spent five years in Spokane, Washington, where he opened healing rooms in an old office building. It is said that over 100,000 documented healings took place during his five years in Spokane. His impact was so profound that Spokane was deemed the healthiest city in America between the years 1915 and 1920 according to government statistics.[4]

In 1996, I spent some time in Spokane researching his life and ministry. I visited his gravesite, asking God to put the same anointing on me for this generation that rested on him. Later, my wife visited this same gravesite before getting the opportunity to meet and pray with his grandson, John G. Lake III.

On this trip, I did some research in the Spokane Library. While reading old newspaper articles of sermons and testimonies found in

The Spokesman Review, I ran across a profound speech given at Lake's funeral. It came from a lady named Irene Poupone, one of Lake's first converts in Spokane. During the ceremony, she said, "When he came to Spokane, he found us in sin, sickness, in poverty and in the grip of despair. We thought the victory was up there, but Dr. Lake taught us it was here."

That's it! That's the answer to our question. There is certainly triumph beyond the grave, but what if we have more power, authority, and victory on earth now than what we had previously assumed? What if the victory is here when we assumed it was up there? What if we are waiting until a coming age to receive something that is available in this present age?

It would prove to be a tragic oversight, robbing us from fulfilling all that we are called to be and accomplish. I don't want to be disappointed one day knowing that my inheritance was current when I assumed it was coming. I don't want to stand before God and see all that I could have had and all I could have done for the Kingdom.

John G. Lake understood that God's Kingdom had come and was fully equipped. He caught a revelation that the current domain of Christ is more powerful than sickness, disease, and darkness. If this be true, imagine how powerful His coming domain will be.

The Kingdom Arriving

He has delivered us from the power of darkness and conveyed us into the kingdom of the Son of His love (Colossians 1:13).

"Convey" means "to be transferred or removed." It is present tense, implying that our citizenship papers have already been transferred out of darkness and into light. Coming into the Kingdom of light is not a future transaction but a current one. This means the Kingdom of God has arrived and is still arriving.

God's great domain is like God Himself—it is, was, and is to come. In the same way that we have been saved, are being saved, and will be saved, so is the Kingdom. Our inheritance is both then and now, and what is laid up for us in the future is already at work in our present.

Sneak Preview

God once gave me a sneak preview of the future when I accompanied my buddy Sean Smith on a ministry trip to South America. The year was 1996, and I was 25 years old. We were ministering at a conference in the city of Cordoba, and the Lord put a special anointing on me at the conference. I had never preached or ministered with these kinds of results. It was surprising but welcomed.

After arriving home to the States, my pastor asked if I would preach at our church. I was counting on that powerful anointing and expecting the great Argentine revival to fall, but it didn't happen. Instead, the meeting fell painfully flat. I was disappointed and humbled. I guess my ministry ship had not come in!

When I asked the Lord what happened, He lovingly told me that the anointing He put on me in Argentina was something that He desired for me in the future, not the present. It was for another season, but He graciously allowed me to taste of it so that I would know what to believe and pray for. God had given me a foretaste to get a taste for a power that was awaiting me.

From time to time God will give us these prophetic previews. They are samples of a coming blessing aimed at whetting our appetites. They are appetizers, foretastes of a future reality, designed to prepare us for the arrival of the main course.

I venture to say that God has given you these same sneak peeks as well. What you thought was a failure in your ministry, a setback in your job, or a regression in your walk may have actually been an invitation to go to a higher realm. Through it, the Lord showed you a reality beyond your current reality and gave you a foretaste of a future reality.

The current Kingdom of God is a prophetic preview of a future glory. Christ wants us to have a foretaste of His kingdom so we get a taste for

His millennial reign. When God gave John a sneak preview of the end times, it was to prepare us for when the Lamb of God returns in a blaze of glory with a heavenly cavalry. All nations will acknowledge Him as the King of kings and the Lord of lords, and a new political era will be established on the earth. This is our inheritance, and our present access to the Kingdom is a promise of this inheritance.

Conclusion

There is coming a day when the Kingdom of Heaven will be on public display, but now it is only open for private viewing. God's laws are celebrated individually and collectively, but one day they will be universally taught and obeyed.[5]

A revolution is stirring. Heaven is approaching. The Kingdom of God has begun. God's throne *is*, and it is present with power. Our future is now. And this is the great paradox of the Kingdom of God.

Endnotes

1. Bill Johnson, *The Supernatural Power of a Transformed Mind* (Shippensburg, PA: Destiny Image, 2005), 41.

2. Roberts Liardon, *God's Generals* (Tulsa, OK: Albury Publishing, 1996), 169.

3. John G. Lake, *Adventures in God* (Tulsa, OK: Harrison House, 1981), 73-74.

4. Roberts Liardon, *God's Generals* (Tulsa, OK: Albury Publishing, 1996), 189.

5. I recommend George Ladd, *The Gospel of the Kingdom* (Grand Rapids, MI: Eerdmans Publishing Co., 1959), for a more comprehensive discussion about the present and future dynamics of the Kingdom.

THE MANIFESTATION OF THE KINGDOM

"And as you go, preach, saying, 'The kingdom of Heaven is at hand.'
Heal the sick, cleanse the lepers, raise the dead, cast out demons.
Freely you have received, freely give."
(Matthew 10:7-8)

S UPERNATURAL power is fundamental to the expansion of the Kingdom. Miracles are not only accessible in the Kingdom but also indispensable to the Great Commission. This section prepares the revolutionary for a life of miracles. It includes: the purpose of signs and wonders; obtaining and releasing Kingdom power; working miracles, healing the sick; casting out demons; influencing culture; unleashing Heaven on earth; and navigating the spiritual dimension.

CHAPTER 6

FIREWORKS

"Jesus of Nazareth was a man accredited by God to you by miracles, wonders and signs, which God did among you through Him, as you yourselves know."
(Acts 2:22 NIV)

BABAOUKARR stood there perplexed as he curiously observed Heaven breaking loose on his village. For the next ninety minutes, he and the rest of the community witnessed a profound supernatural occurrence taking place in their own backyard. They testified to malaria leaving, spines realigning, deaf ears opening, shortened legs growing, head and stomach pains disappearing, and mutes speaking their name for the first time. This all took place in June of 2005 in Sanyang, a small town in Gambia, Africa.

I met Babaoukarr on our second evangelistic trip to the Gambia while handing out tracts in his neighborhood. He looked to be about 22 years old and spoke English well for one living in a primarily Mandinka-speaking community. This rural village had no established church, and this was our first visit to the seaside town. As we walked from tin-roofed huts to living room–sized concrete houses, I invited Babaoukarr to the afternoon meeting. Soon, he and about 100 villagers gathered under a big spreading tree to listen to the message.[1]

Matthew Gonzales, a powerful campus evangelist and one of our team members, preached that afternoon through translation. Most joined in the singing and respectfully stood by listening to the message, but only a few responded in faith toward Christ. That all changed when the Holy Spirit showed up and showed off!

Matt had a word of knowledge that we were to pray for people who had pain in their feet. As the word went forth, six or seven responded. Minutes later six or seven were instantly healed! These healings started a snowball effect of bold faith. People bum-rushed us for prayer, and God started performing miracle after miracle for more than an hour.

After the Holy Spirit smoke had cleared, we witnessed four mute people talking and four deaf ears open. Countless backs, stomachs, heads, chests, knees, and the like were healed. There were so many healings taking place at one time that we could not keep pace with all the testimonies. I have been in meetings where a strong healing presence was manifested, but this was an outbreak of miracles. It was unusual. It was exhilarating. It was real. Just about all those we prayed for were instantly and miraculously healed.[2]

In the middle of the power surge, the Holy Spirit began to tug on Babaoukarr's heart. He came to me requesting prayer. He explained that he had dislocated his shoulders in a car accident years ago and lived with continual head pain. He showed me the gash on his head, and I observed his displaced shoulder blades.

I asked Babaoukarr what he would do if Jesus healed him, and he said he would praise Him. I asked him if Jesus healed him, would he renounce all other gods and serve only Christ. He replied, "Yes, gladly." So we prayed, and God gloriously and beautifully healed him. All pain left him instantly, and his shoulder blades and spine popped back into place. Laughing and crying, he humbly confessed his sins and placed his trust in Christ Jesus for salvation. His friend, who was observing the entire encounter, was convinced of the claims of Christ and also was soundly converted.

These events sparked a miraculous *change* reaction, the miracle of a changed heart. One by one, Gambians who had experienced a miracle or had witnessed their family members being healed stepped forward to submit their lives and families to Jesus Christ. Individually, we led each one to Christ.

Re-mystifying the Gospel

...the spirit of Him who raised Jesus from the dead dwells in you...(Romans 8:11).

If you believe in Christ you believe in miracles, because He is a sign and a wonder (see Isa. 9:6, Luke 2:34). Our spiritual DNA is profoundly supernatural. Do you realize that your faith rests squarely on the miraculous—the miracle of the empty tomb? Without it, our faith is futile and our preaching is vain. Western Christianity has tried to demystify the gospel, but to deny the supernatural is to deny the very work and nature of Christ in us.

Through the power of the empty tomb, diseases are cured, demons are terrorized, and even death is defeated. Now that the rock has been rolled away, you and I have been invited to join those throughout history who have witnessed the supernatural workings of God. Not only are miracles essential to our history, but they are also the spiritual technology of our future.

The Holy Spirit spoke to me clearly one day, saying, "It is time for fireworks." Unsure what He meant, I questioned, "Fireworks?" He said, "Yes, works of fire!" Then I knew what He meant. He was talking about the miraculous.

Fireworks were invented by the ancient Chinese and were thought to chase away evil spirits. By the fourteenth century, the Europeans used them as weaponry, but now they are mostly enjoyed as entertainment.[3] The fiery works of God are not for pleasure or for show. God forbid we should exploit them to raise more funds for our ministry or use them to bask in the limelight of the anointing. They are intended to be instruments of spiritual war that ward off devils.

Now is the time for fireworks. There is coming a day when it will be common to see blind eyes opened, deaf ears restored, wheelchairs abandoned, cancer removed, AIDS eradicated, Down's syndrome reversed, and the dead raised. I have a personal vision to see conjoined twins suddenly and miraculously morphed apart into two bodies by the spoken word of God.

In Acts 19, Paul worked unusual miracles. As this Kingdom age progresses we will see extraordinary Kingdom manifestations taking place en masse. There is coming a day when even the most severe diseases will not stand before the people of God.

Signs and wonders serve a strategic purpose. They should neither be our goal nor our neglect, but they are an indispensable means toward a greater end.

A Means for Faith

...Unless you people see signs and wonders, you will by no means believe (John 4:48).

"By no means?" Was Jesus serious? This statement is not necessarily a critique or a compliment. It is an observation. Signs and wonders are a legitimate means for faith in Christ. Like Thomas, many people will not believe without a visible sign, and this should excite us.

I think we have been too harsh on poor Thomas. He simply would not settle for a secondhand account of the resurrection. He wanted a personal encounter with the risen Lord. This is not only admirable but also necessary. When Jesus suddenly appeared and beckoned him to experience the reality of His resurrection firsthand, Thomas cried, *"My Lord and my God!"* (See John 20:24-29.)

There are atheists and skeptics today who will *by no means* believe without a sign and a wonder, and I don't get the idea that this exasperates God like we think it does. After all, Jesus obliged Bartimaeus, Nicodemus, Nathaniel, Mary, the centurion, the man at the pool, the famished crowd, the woman with the issue of blood, and the disciples on transfiguration mountain. While the greater blessing awaits those who, having never seen, still believe, the supernatural plays a pivotal role in unlocking the unbelieving heart toward faith in Christ. Even our largest churches, most compassionate deeds, and most aggressive evangelism campaigns cannot accomplish what a miracle can. It alone carries with it a means for faith.

Thomas was changed forever by this one encounter. History reveals that he not only lived for Christ but also died for Him. I happened to visit the city of Chennai in India where Thomas was believed to have been brutally speared to death for his faith. He was a true champion of the gospel. What was it that caused him to change his moniker from a doubter to a martyr? It was an undeniable, supernatural encounter with the Risen Lord.

A harvest awaits those who will partner with the Holy Spirit and demonstrate to the unbeliever the power of the Kingdom. You are the sign, and I am the wonder that points them to Christ. Many will still doubt, and not all will believe, but unquestionably some will.

Stand in Awe of God

For the Father loves the Son, and shows Him all things that He
Himself does; and He will show Him greater works than these,
that you may marvel (John 5:20).

God is truly supernatural, meaning He has a superior nature. It is just as easy for Him to perform a miracle as it is to move a mountain, create a galaxy, or suspend the laws of physics. When God colors outside the lines, it causes us to marvel, and He desires that we do.

At times, God purposely wows us. The burning bush, the plagues of Egypt, and the glory on Mount Sinai are vivid examples. When this occurs, His power should cause all to admire Him. Unfortunately, the Israelites did the opposite. They worshipped a false glory when they should have been standing in awe of God's. The purpose of a sign and a wonder is that we would contemplate and behold the wonders of God.

I once attended a wedding, and the father of the bride was complaining about his back. He was not a follower of Christ, and he explained to me how much and for how long he had been in pain. After I laid hands on him, he was astounded that the pain had left. During the reception, he would come up to me periodically, so overjoyed and in awe of God. He was as giddy as a school boy, and this was before the wine was served!

The *greater works* mentioned here are the same greater works that Jesus promised later when He said, "*...He who believes in Me, the works that I do he will do also; and greater works than these he will do, because I go to My Father*" (John 14:12). With Heaven's authorization, we can expect to operate in works that are greater in number and greater in magnitude than even those found in the New Testament. The Book of Acts is not our high-water mark. It is our history. We have yet to walk in these greater works, but there is coming a day in the Kingdom when we will.

Jesus Is God's Messenger

> *...the works which the Father has given Me to finish—the very works that I do—bear witness of Me, that the Father has sent Me* (John 5:36).

When God does something spectacular, we tend to become overly enamored with the person whom He works the miracle through. We assume the Lord must surely approve of his or her lifestyle and doctrine, but this is not always the case. Signs and wonders done in Jesus' name do not necessarily prove that the minister is endorsed by God, but rather they prove that the name in which the miracles are done is endorsed by God.

A word of knowledge or a healed bladder does not to validate my anointing, my ministry, or my position with the Father. Instead, it validates Christ's ministry, confirms His position, and is proof that He is God's anointed messenger. Without question, the purity of my character and doctrine will eventually affect God's power flowing through me, but not always immediately. The enemy will often wait to expose us until our secret sin wreaks maximum havoc on innocent lives.

> ...men of Israel, why do you marvel at this? Or why look so intently at us, as though by our own power or godliness we had made this man walk?...His name [Jesus], through faith in His name, has made this man strong...(Acts 3:12,16).

The only way I can take credit for a miracle is when I perform it in my own name. If I work a miracle in the name of Jeff Rostocil, then perhaps my morals and theology are validated, but the last time I checked I couldn't even heal a nagging hangnail on a good day.

Jesus Is One With the Father

> If I do not do the works of My Father, do not believe Me; but if I do, though you do not believe Me, believe the works, that you may know and believe that the Father is in Me, and I in Him (John 10:37-38).

Miracles are proof that Jesus is more than a good teacher or a Jewish theologian. They point to His deity, and the world will be held accountable for what they witness through our lives. Signs and wonders will take the witness stand on Judgment Day to testify against those who saw but refused to believe.

Some fear that the supernatural will cause people to put their faith in an experience rather than the Word of God, but isn't the Word of God our model and motivation for faith in miracles? The Bible is to lead us into an experiential knowledge of Christ, not into an academic one. Jesus encouraged those who could not believe in His words to trust in His works, for they would point them to the Word of God. We should not be alarmed by an experiential faith grounded in God's Word, but rather we should be wary of those who teach the Word from only a theoretical faith.

This does not mean we should blindly follow all who work miracles. Apparently, the Pharisees could prophesy and exorcize demons (see

John 11:45-47; Matt. 12:27; Acts 19:13). Additionally, false prophets prophesy, cast out demons, and work wonders in the name of Jesus (see Matt. 7:15-23). What we must ask is: "Does the miracle glorify Christ and honor God's commands?" If it does, it is good fruit. If it does not, we should discard it. The gift of discernment will prove to be a crucial gift as we approach the end of this age.

The Great Commission

"...Go into all the world and preach the gospel...He who believes and is baptized will be saved...these signs will follow those who believe: In My name they will cast out demons... speak with new tongues...take up serpents...if they drink anything deadly, it will by no means hurt them...lay hands on the sick, and they will recover." ...And they went out and preached everywhere, the Lord working with them and confirming the word through the accompanying signs (Mark 16:15-20).

The Great Commission widens the Kingdom because it establishes the lordship of Christ in the human heart. In this passage, we learn that signs and wonders follow four specific activities:

1. The preaching of the gospel: *"...Go into all the world and preach the gospel to every creature"* (Mark 16:15).

God still uses *"the foolishness of preaching"* (1 Cor. 1:21 KJV) as the foremost tool to populate the Kingdom. His anointing on the preached word is always purposed toward Kingdom objectives, and signs and wonders are meant to accompany it. All too often, though, our preaching is too vain, our expectation is too low, and our prayers are too safe. We are guilty, myself included, of preaching feel-good sermons and praying tax-loophole prayers. However, a flabby gospel or as Bonhoeffer calls it, "cheap grace," is usually not conducive to the conviction of the Holy Spirit.

Somehow we have abandoned the message of the Kingdom for more convenient truths, but is there a more profound and relevant message to the human soul than the good news of Jesus Christ? Jesus is our foundation and our pinnacle, our origin and our destination, our beginning and our end. We should not look past Him, but look to go higher, deeper, and further in Him.

If we want results like the New Testament, we must preach a New Testament gospel and contend for the faith of our forefathers. Preaching the word does not automatically ensure that miracles will take place, but it does make them a viable option. And if these signs never follow my ministry, I am compelled to ask myself: "Am I preaching the gospel?"

2. Baptism: *"He who believes and is baptized will be saved..."* (Mark 16:16).

We've shied away from emphasizing the importance of baptism, but it is a necessary ingredient in discipling the nations. Like the Ethiopian eunuch, one of the first acts of obedience of every convert should be water baptism.

3. Faith: *"These signs will follow those who believe..."* (Mark 16:17).

The gospel of the Kingdom is designed to be active, not passive. Not only should we have active faith in Christ, but we should also have faith that signs will follow the preaching of the Word.

4. The Name of Jesus: *"...In My Name they will..."* (Mark 16:17)

A beggar crippled from birth asked Peter and John for money as they entered the Temple. Peter looked him in the eye and said, *"Silver and gold I do not have, but what I do have I give to you: In the name of Jesus Christ of Nazareth, rise up and walk"* (Acts 3:6). When the man did just that, pandemonium broke loose. People went berserk, for they all knew this man and his condition. They praised God, and the former paraplegic would not shut up about it. He refused to let go of Peter and John. Finally, Peter stood up and explained to the throngs of people what had just happened. He preached Christ to them, many believed, and not surprisingly the apostles were arrested because of it (see Acts 3).

For better or for worse, we emit what we contain. What was it that Peter had to give to this poor beggar? He possessed the Name of Jesus and the keys to a powerful Kingdom. This one miracle was the catalyst for a holy uprising in Jerusalem. It seems the Name and Person of Jesus Christ within us have the ability to shape the world around us, and maybe revival in our churches, communities, and campuses is just one miracle away.

Conclusion

It's unnatural to not have an appetite for the miraculous. Don't apologize or be embarrassed that you crave supernatural expressions of your faith, and don't be discouraged when miracles don't happen at will. Your hunger and faith for the supernatural are sure indications the Kingdom has come to you.

Life is meant to be a continual and never-ending revelation of the Lamb of God. Don't stop at your current revelation of Christ. Add to your pursuit—Jesus the Wonder Worker. The greatest miracle in the history of the world took place in a cemetery, which means that even in our darkest hour the Risen Lord shows up. Our fiercest hour seems to be His finest. Keep pressing on.

Endnotes

1. This was our second evangelistic trip to Gambia in just over a year. On our first outreach, Meljoné and I and a team of seven ardent college students witnessed to just about everything that moved— in churches, airports, hospitals, at the docks, on street corners, in the marketplace, with store owners, and even on top a van on a crowded ferry surrounded by hundreds of listening Muslims.

   On that first trip, God worked mighty miracles in both the meetings and in the open air. We were given the opportunity to bring the gospel to a small, unreached people group on the northern banks of the country. This remote community has no running water or electricity; they live in thatched-roofed bamboo huts and grind their bread with sticks and stones. After we presented the story of the gospel to them, I am very pleased to report that every single person present was converted, starting with the chief of the village. We watched them as they broke off their fetishes and invited Christ to be the Lord of their village. We wept. Heaven rejoiced. It was a day of great victory.

In another city, we conducted revival meetings and open-air outreaches. We witnessed profound conversions and mighty manifestations. Knees, backs, skin conditions, bleeding disorders, mute people, and several cases of malaria were among the healing testimonies.

2. One man approached us with his new pack of cigarettes and matches. He gave them to us, saying that Jesus had set him free and delivered him from his smoking addiction. He testified that Christ had also healed his back. We discovered that those who were not instantly healed that day were those who wore a fetish given (or sold) to them by the witchdoctor. When they removed the juju, renounced its hold, and put their faith in Christ, they were set free from their pain or disease. Those who did not renounce and remove their ties to witchcraft remained in bondage.

3. Microsoft Encarta Encyclopedia, computer software, version Deluxe 2000 (Microsoft Corporation, 1999).

CHAPTER 7

FULLY LOADED

"My speech and my preaching were not with persuasive words of human wisdom, but in demonstration of the Spirit and of power, that your faith should not be in the wisdom of men but in the power of God."
(1 Corinthians 2:4-5)

ONE messenger consumed with a burning desire for Kingdom exploits has the power to transform an entire city. Just ask the Samaritans.

After the stoning of Stephen, the early church experienced widespread persecution at the hands of a Pharisee named Saul. Men were beaten, women were thrown into prison, and some were even put to death. Forced to leave their homes, the first-century believers all became missionaries as they scattered throughout the Middle East. Yet, even under these severe conditions the Word of God continued to spread like wildfire.

Luke records that while the rank and file believers *gossiped* the good news everywhere they went, Philip *proclaimed* Christ in Samaria. Paraplegics walked, the blind saw, demons were evicted, multitudes believed, and all hung on the evangelist's every word. Even an influential sorcerer named Simon, nicknamed "The Great Power of God," renounced his ways and was baptized when he witnessed the miraculous displays of power. Scripture records that there was great joy in the city (see Acts 8:1-25).

Are you curious to know what Philip said to the crowds that sparked such a great revival and attracted that kind of power? Luke tells us, saying that Philip *"preached the things concerning the Kingdom of God and the name of Jesus Christ"* (Acts 8:12).

The Threefold Commission

The miracle at Samaria was not an aberration, and Philip is not the exception. Whenever the Lord sends out disciples, He demonstrates how to do it first and then equips us with the necessary power to get the job done.

> *Then Jesus went about all the cities and villages, teaching in their synagogues, preaching the gospel of the kingdom, and healing every sickness and every disease among the people* (Matthew 9:35).

> *And when He had called His twelve disciples to Him, He gave them power over unclean spirits, to cast them out, and to heal all kinds of sickness and all kinds of disease* (Matthew 10:1).

> *He sent them to preach the kingdom of God and to heal the sick* (Luke 9:2).

> *Go your way; behold, I send you out as lambs among wolves. ...And heal the sick there, and say to them, "The Kingdom of God has come near to you"* (Luke 10:3,9).

As Kingdom emissaries, we have been given a threefold job assignment: Preach the Kingdom, heal the sick, and cast out demons. The commission of Christ is never without these three elements. When my wife and I prepare a team for an evangelistic outreach, we endeavor to train them in these three areas. Honestly, this is our mandate when we consider evangelism, and it should be our expectation. If we will prepare ourselves and our missionaries in the way that Jesus did, we shouldn't be surprised when God begins to save, heal, and deliver the nations.

These three activities are symbiotic in nature, meaning one cannot be completely fulfilled without the other. So I want to look at each one in greater depth and offer practical tips on how to accomplish these in the marketplace.

Preaching

God is a master communicator. He *commanded* the universe to order, *conversed* with Adam in the Garden, and initiated *communication* with him after the fall (see Gen. 1:3; 6:9-22). He *called* Abraham out of the land of Ur, *spoke* to Moses face to face, and *commissioned* Jeremiah as a prophet (see Gen. 12:1-14; Exod. 4:11-12; Deut. 8:3; Ps. 33:6-9). From the very beginning, God opened lines of communication before humanity ever considered pursuing Him.

With the exception of Esther, every book of the Bible contains meaningful dialogue between Heaven and earth. Even the Scriptures themselves are a written communiqué of the Father. God's nature is so indelibly linked with speech that He named His only begotten Son the *Living Word of God* (see John 1:1-2; Rev. 19:10).

The call to the Kingdom is a call to communicate, both with God and with people. You and I are designed to be God's sound system on earth, and it is essential that every minister be well instructed in the Kingdom message.

> *...Every scribe instructed concerning the kingdom of Heaven is like a householder who brings out of his treasure things new and old* (Matthew 13:52).

> *...Let the dead bury their own dead, but you go and preach the kingdom of God* (Luke 9:60).

The early church fathers were schooled in the message of the Kingdom. James spoke of the Kingdom (see James 2:5). The writer of Hebrews elaborates on the Kingdom (see Heb. 12:28). Paul preached, taught, and testified of the Kingdom often (see Acts 28:23; 30-31). The Book of Acts records him marching into the synagogue of Ephesus and arguing persuasively about the Kingdom for three months (see Acts 19:8). He did something similar in Lystra, Iconium, Antioch, and Rome (see Acts 14:21-22; 20:25; 28:23; 30-31). The only gospel the early disciples knew was the gospel of the Kingdom, and now this torch has been passed on to us.

When I was younger, I observed two kinds of preachers. The first were those who displayed true humility and brokenness. They were not afraid to cry in front of their audience or share their weakness. Their compassion was contagious. These fathers stood as timeless models of character and integrity. To their own admission, however, they weren't the most dynamic ministers. Many had never been exposed to the power of God nor operated in the gifts of the Spirit. They were remarkable leaders but felt awkward at the moving of the Spirit.

The second group of preachers walked in unusual power and could prophesy with pinpoint accuracy. Miracles of healing regularly accompanied their ministry. They could communicate with incredible persuasion and turn a phrase like no other, but all too often they were skimpy on holiness. Some treated their wives like a used car, trading them in for a newer model; others were closet alcoholics or caught manipulating widows out of money.

I used to wonder: What kind of preacher will I be? Will I be humble or powerful? Will I walk in the gifts of the Spirit or the fruit of the Spirit? Then it dawned on me. They are not mutually exclusive. I don't have to choose between the two. In the Kingdom, I can be powerful *and* humble. I can be anointed *and* integral. It is not either/or but both and more. This has been my pursuit. Like a double-barreled shotgun, the world needs both and the correct answer is not *A* or *B*; it is *All the Above*. God is offering us all that the Above has to offer.

In your communication of the gospel, strive for purity *and* power. Without power, we cannot successfully accomplish the Great Commission. Without purity, we will not sustain the power of God long term.

Kingdom Communication Tips

1. ***Engage Heaven.*** Engaging Heaven is more important than engaging our audiences, because favor with the listener is useless if we have no favor with God. Only He has the ability to change a heart. What good is the applause of humans if we do not have the applause of Heaven? What good is it to earn the respect of our peers but lose the respect of God? We become credible witnesses for Christ only by gaining credibility with the One we represent. The preacher must know how to pray and access the presence of God.

2. ***Set yourself on fire.*** Reinhard Bonnke tells a comical story about a confrontation he had with satan at one of his evangelistic campaigns in Africa. At that time, he had a 10,000-person revival tent, and it was pitched in Greenvalley, South Africa. A powerful African storm was threatening to interrupt the revival and destroy the tent. As the storm approached, he felt led of the Holy Spirit to point his finger to the blackened sky and rebuke the storm. He exclaimed, "Satan, in the name of Jesus, I want to talk to you. Devil, if you destroy this tent of mine, I'm going to trust God for another one three times the size of this one."

Something unbelievable suddenly occurred. The clouds parted, and the thunderstorm took a detour around the tent. They went on with the meetings and saw thousands saved, healed, and delivered. After the revival, Reinhard spoke with satan again, just so he wouldn't get any ideas, saying, "Devil, in the name of Jesus, I want to talk to you once more. Although you withdrew the wind and you withdrew the rain, that does not mean that I have made an agreement with you. I will still build a bigger tent anyway." And indeed he did![1]

I once read where the preachers of old would retreat into the wilderness and remain completely silent for days, even weeks at a time. When they entered a city to preach, the word was like fire shut up in their bones and the zeal of God would burn through them. Charles Wesley said, "Set yourself on fire and people will come for miles to watch you burn." Get ignited. While we are not all called to speak from a stage or a tent, we are all called to speak from the platform that God has given us.

Fathers, mothers, teachers, doctors, employers, leaders—in your sphere of authority, you are an anointed communicator of the Kingdom.

3. **Be creative.** In naming the animals, Adam's job was to create new words to communicate to the world in which he lived. Likewise, our creativity in expressing truth glorifies our Creator. You and I are diplomats of Heaven, translating the language of Heaven into the language of earth. Speak the dialect of your audience. Offer them a solution to their circumstance and tap into the cry of this generation. It is often found in their music.

The great artist Pablo Picasso once said, "My mother said to me, 'If you become a soldier you'll become a general, if you become a monk you'll end up the pope.' Instead, I became a painter and wound up as Picasso."[2]

Don't be afraid to think outside the box. Michelangelo, Shakespeare, Handel, Pascal, Van Gogh, Tennyson, Churchill, Frost, C.S. Lewis, and Martin Luther King Jr. are examples of great artists who have proven this world can be revolutionized by inspired communicators who allow the conviction of God to anoint their pens, direct their tongues, and inspire their work.

Healing the Sick

A leper came to Jesus, knelt down, and begged Him, "*If You are willing, You can make me clean*" (Mark 1:40). This was a monumental event because the leper was asking the very question we all eventually ask. He did not doubt Jesus' *ability* to heal, but rather His *desire* to heal. He asked, "Is it Your will to heal me? I know You can do it, but do You care enough to heal the likes of me?"

Jesus resolved the issue once and for all when He touched this outcast and said, "*I am willing; be cleansed*" (Mark 1:41). This one phrase settled it. The heart wish of Christ was, is, and will always be to heal the hurt and destroy the pain of those He loves. This is why in many places all who were sick and demonized were set free (see Matt. 4:23-24; 8:16; 12:15;

14:35-36; Mark 1:32-34; Luke 4:40-41; 6:19; 9:6,11; Acts 5:16; 10:38; and 28:9). As F.F. Bruce said, "Men more easily believe in miraculous power than in miraculous love."[3]

The great healing revivalists of old taught us that faith begins where the will of God is known. If this is true, our effectiveness in healing the sick is directly related to our revelation of Christ the Healer. When we are unsure about the will of God, it is harder to pray with confidence, but boldness comes when we are convinced that Jesus desires to heal the person standing in front of us.

Healing is a byproduct of the Kingdom and is available whenever the gospel is shared. I will never forget the miracle I witnessed while street witnessing one night near Haight and Ashbury Streets in San Francisco. We came upon a group of people congregated in an alleyway and noticed a couple huddled in the corner under a blanket. They told us they were homeless and had been living on the streets for several years. After sharing Christ with them, they gladly submitted their lives to Him.

When we asked how we could specifically pray for them, the husband explained that his wife had a condition in her legs that left her paralyzed. For three years he had been carrying her around from homeless shelter to shelter. When we heard this, we all gathered around her and spoke the word of the Lord. As we helped her to her feet, God performed a miracle right before our eyes. We watched her emaciated legs gain strength as she marched down the street with hands lifted heavenward, praising God. The look of exuberance on her face was priceless. Many of the other street people stood in wonder, as they were well aware of her condition. It was an awesome miracle. Needless to say, we preached Christ with extra boldness that night.

Jesus is committed to healing the sick. Nearly 20 percent of the gospels are devoted to the healing ministry of Christ, and over 60 percent of His ministry involved healing and deliverance. This is far more than any other activity. If you are a minister who does not spend a good percentage of your time ministering to the sick, what are you waiting for? You are missing out on all the fun.

One day the Lord invited me to dream with Him, and since then I have carried an outlandish vision in my heart. I was embarrassed to share it openly until recently. The dream is this: I want all disease completely banned and eradicated from the planet and to see every person walking in divine health. Preposterous pipe dream? Perhaps. Impossible for God? Not on your life.

Wouldn't it be amazing if sickness was simply not a factor for the human race? I can't begin to tell you how the Lord intends to accomplish this, but I believe this dream is from the heart of God.

What is your dream? What impossible mission has God placed inside of your heart? If we are going to be people of faith, why not believe for something that only God could do and that would cause all to glorify Christ? Why believe for the inevitable when you can believe for the impossible?

I am convinced there is coming a day in the Kingdom when this dream will become reality. Scripture seems to indicate that all disease will one day be eliminated from God's earthly kingdom, and I want to be a part of the company of people that helps promote it (see Isa. 33:24; 35:5-6). D. Thomas Lancaster writes, "We would do well to let the rule of the coming Kingdom dictate how the servants of the King live now."[4] Knowing that sickness will not be a part of the future kingdom indicates that ministering to the sick is part of Kingdom living.

Tips for Healing

1. Release healing. Have you ever noticed that Jesus and the disciples did not pray for the sick? They carried healing with them. In the marketplace, we are commissioned to *"heal the sick"* (see Matt. 10:8; Luke 9:2; 10:9). It is one thing to pray for healing; it is quite another to declare it. In evangelism, speak the healing word and declare it. Seek to release healing by verbally addressing the injured body part and declaring Scripture over it.

2. Build faith. A testimony of healing has the ability to embolden our faith as well as theirs. This happened with my wife and me on our first date. She was complaining of back pain and told me that she had injured her lower back several years ago while performing a ballet piece. When we checked the length of her legs, one was an inch shorter than the other. As I shared Scripture and a testimony, our faith soared, and her leg grew out right in front of our eyes. The pain left and both legs were equal in length. That day God healed her back, and He had mine. I suggest bringing the Holy Spirit with you on your dates. Evidently, it made quite an impression.

3. Cure with care. Even when Jesus was physically and emotionally exhausted, Scripture records that he was *"moved with compassion"* for the crowds (see Matt. 9:36; 14:14; Mark 1:41). If compassion fueled Jesus to heal all who were sick, why would He neglect those who cry out to Him in their suffering today? Our love for people must grow stronger than our insecurities and inhibitions. When we tap into the compassionate heart of Christ, we invariably tap into a realm of power.

4. Don't panic if nothing happens or the person gets worse. Four things can happen when you minister to the sick. First, the person is instantly healed. This is always the most exhilarating and enjoyable. Second, the healing process begins. Sometimes a person may experience an initial decrease in pain, but not a complete release. Jesus said to *"lay hands on the sick and they shall recover"* (Mark 16:18). Often the recovery process begins with a touch. As we minister to them, their healing is set in motion, and over time the body gradually recovers. Third, the pain increases or moves to another place in their body. When this happens, don't panic. The sickness is usually demonically linked. Cast out a tormenting spirit of affliction and infirmity, and you should see some positive results. Fourth, nothing happens. For this I have no good answer. Sometimes it can be an indication that the illness is spiritually rooted or that there is a block to the healing (such as fear, rejection, or unforgiveness). If this is the case, remove the block and often healing will occur.

5. Don't give up. Reading the accounts of men and women used powerfully in healing, most started out with little success. In fact, some even died of their conditions. God will often test us to see if we take the credit or the blame for the miracle. He wants to know if our compassion and obedience are strong enough to press past the question of why some do not get healed.

I was ministering in southern India when a man approached us and asked that we come pray for his wife. He explained that she had broken both her hips and was unable to move. We agreed and followed him to his house. When we walked through the door, I could smell death in the room. This frail woman looked like she weighed no more than 80 pounds and was sitting in a chair in the dark. Her body was covered with flies, as she didn't even have the strength to swat them away. Our hearts sank.

Our team quickly huddled around her, quoted Scripture, prayed, and laid hands on her. We lifted her out of her chair and walked her around the room, but no signs of healing occurred. We cried; we pleaded; we worshipped. We gave it our all, but she was still in agony and seemed to have no will to live.

We left that day having seen no great miracle. On the ride back to our hotel, I never felt so dejected. We had prayed for countless people on that trip and had not seen one of them healed. The disappointment was almost unbearable, and a sense of failure began to creep in. Why did I even bother in the first place? It hurt too much. While we were determined to still minister to the sick, I couldn't help but think of all those who were not healed.

Three months after we had arrived back in the States, I received a message from the missionary. He said the very woman we had prayed for made a miraculous recovery. She was healed and had been walking around as normal. When I heard the news, I dropped to my knees, and I learned a very crucial lesson that day. Even if you don't see instant results, keep praying, keep believing. You never know what God may be doing behind the scenes.

On another occasion, I was praying with a woman who was 104 years old. She was a mighty intercessor, but cancer had tragically confined her to a wheelchair and taken her eyesight. I could see the cancer eating away at her cheek and mouth. Her prayer request was not for healing, but that she would leave a spiritual legacy for her children by not dying of cancer.

At age 105, she did indeed die, but not from cancer. She died of old age and left a powerful heritage of faith for her children. There was no quit in this mighty Deborah. Her spirit exclaimed, "Oh, no you don't, devil. I may be down but I am not out!" She refused to give up.

Casting out Demons

Don't you get the idea that Jesus had a personal vendetta against satan? Scripture records that He destroyed "the works of the devil" and "made a public spectacle" of principalities (see 1 John 3:8; Col. 2:15). Our Lord seems to take extra pleasure in healing the sick, raising the dead, casting out demons, and demolishing the works of darkness, and it is perfectly acceptable for you to have the same attitude. Take out your frustrations on your adversary by plundering his camp. Heal the sick. Raise the dead. Cast out demons and be furious at the devil.

> ...*Every kingdom divided against itself is brought to desolation.... If Satan casts out Satan, he is divided against himself. How then will his kingdom stand? But if I cast out demons by the Spirit of God, surely the kingdom of God has come upon you* (Matthew 12:25-26; 28).

Christ's dominion over demons proves that the power of the *age to come* is more powerful than the *spirit of the age*. When the disciples reported that even the demons were subject to them in His name, Jesus said, "*I saw Satan fall like lightning from Heaven*" (Luke 10:18). Satan's power is diminished as we preach, and the work of deliverance is clear evidence that the Kingdom of God has come.

When dealing with demons, the most critical information to know is your authority. Be diligent to exercise your God-given authority, yet do not assume more authority than you have been given. This takes courage and humility. We only have dominion in the places where He sends us and within our God-given domain.

When I visit a region, I do not attempt to pull down the strongholds over a city. Those who seek to engage a principality over a territory should proceed with considerable caution. Proverbs 20:18 warns about waging war without wisdom, and we must choose our spiritual battles wisely. There are many needless casualties of war because well-meaning intercessors leave their spheres of authority, go up to the second Heaven, pick a fight with a high-ranking demon, pray unauthorized prayers, and fight unauthorized wars

An unauthorized war is one that our Commander-in-Chief is neither fighting nor sanctioning. We must be careful to engage only in warfare that Christ is calling us to, for if we step out of God's protection it will negatively affect those that we mean to cover.

> *The heaven, even the heavens, are the Lord's; but the earth He has given to the children of men* (Psalm 115:16).

The battle has never been for the heavens but always for the earth, and this earth is our sphere of authority. We can cast out demons that tread upon the earth, but going into the heavens is God's arena. Scripture does not authorize this type of warfare. Moreover, a principality cannot be cast out of its place. It must be wrestled with (see Eph. 6:12).

The New Testament reveals that principalities were created through and for Christ, and it appears they must submit to the activity of the people with whom they govern (see Col. 1:16). If people act righteously, the land will be blessed. If people act treacherously, the land will be cursed. When the sin that empowers a principality is repented of, the strongman is debilitated. Additionally, when lower ranking demons are expelled from that region, the ruling spirit is weakened.

Preaching the gospel of the Kingdom with signs and wonders exposes demonic strongholds and allows people to break free from demonic oppression. When unbelievers repent of their lifestyle and expel their demons, the principality they are empowering loses its influence over them and the land.

The gospels reveal that the ministry of healing and deliverance work hand in hand. You will eventually run into demons if you minister to the sick long enough, but don't be alarmed. When a person manifests a demon, it simply means that the Anointed One is present to deliver.

Tips for Deliverance

1. Remove all legal access. The devil has access to every area of darkness. He and his cohorts will not leave until they lose their right to stay, and even when they no longer have legal ground they often will not leave until confronted. They are trespassers and trash-passers. Your job is to revoke their license and enforce the law. Make sure that demonized people want to be free and are willing to walk away from their sins. If they do not want to be free, their freedom will not remain and their bondage may only increase (see Luke 11:24-26). Get the person who is bound to confess his or her sin and renounce the activity that is feeding the stronghold. I have found that people receive deliverance in the same way they receive salvation—through repentance and faith.

2. Don't be flippant or afraid. Avoid underestimating or over-inflating the power of satan. The devil is described as cunning, so it is proper to maintain a healthy militaristic respect for the enemy (see Gen. 3:1). Satan is not to blame for everything, but we cannot be ignorant of his work. When we believe that everything is caused by the devil, it glorifies the work of darkness and forces us to take our eyes off Jesus. When we believe that nothing is caused by the devil, it leaves us vulnerable to his vices.

3. Keep your eyes open when you minister to someone who is demonized. This is not only for your protection, but also because the nature of the attack can sometimes be determined through the person's actions and expressions. I once ministered to a teenage girl who had ten demons in her. As she fell to the ground, she flailed her arms and beat herself with her fists. As it turned out, she been physically abused as a child and had recently been cutting herself. The spirits of abuse and suicide were manifesting, and the nature of the oppression could be discerned by her actions. We had to individually cast all ten out of her, but she was gloriously freed and filled with the Holy Spirit. Sometimes you can't discern the spirit naturally, so I've found it helpful to also ask the Holy Spirit for words of knowledge during the deliverance session.

4. Stay clean. Deliverance ministry is not for the compromising believer. You cannot defeat an external enemy that you internally entertain. If we attempt to cast out demons that we ourselves secretly flirt with, we may find ourselves like the seven sons of Sceva—stripped, embarrassed, and exposed. Seek intimacy with Christ. Satan will build strongholds in our lives in the places we refuse to allow the Lord to be our stronghold.

5. Fast and pray. Jesus said certain kinds of demons are expelled only through prayer and fasting (see Matt. 9:29). Make fasting a regular part of your walk with Christ. I have found value in both the discipline of fasting and extended fasting. *Disciplined fasts* are shorter, consistent fasts, like a meal a day or two days a week. Usually, I will fast for discipline when my spirit needs sharpening or I am preparing for a time of ministry. *Extended fasts* are fasts that cover multiple days and weeks. These typically target something specific that God is highlighting. I generally do not begin an extended fast unless I feel prompted by the Lord. Prayer and fasting have played significant roles in any advances I have made in the anointing, including deliverance ministry.

The Secret to Signs and Wonders

*Then He appointed twelve, that they might be **with Him** and that He might send them out to preach, and to have power to heal sicknesses and to cast out demons* (Mark 3:14-15).

Our first ministry is to be with Jesus. We tend to elevate the call to ministry, but ministry is just a fancy word for serving. We serve Christ much like Mary of Bethany did—sitting at His feet and pouring our love upon Him. Like meat marinating in sauce, our souls become thoroughly saturated with His savor as we wait on Him. We are the meat, and His presence is the special sauce.

The secret to signs and wonders is this: there is no secret! Get around the Anointed One and His anointing will rub off on you. Once the ministry of waiting on God is established, then we can launch boldly into a life of miracles.

The power of God is not often automatic. We must appreciate, activate, appropriate, cultivate, and celebrate it in order to demonstrate it. Go on a prayer retreat. Learn from those who walk in power. Meditate on the words and miracles of Jesus. Study the lives of the apostles and prophets. Educate yourself in the things of the Spirit. Minister to every sick person you can. God's power is more caught than taught.

Conclusion

A surprising miracle occurred immediately after the revival in Samaria. Saul of Tarsus had a blinding encounter with the King of Light. He abruptly abandoned his assault against the Way and became the greatest communicator it has ever seen. Saul the persecutor became Paul the apostle, and I believe this is prophetic as we enter the approaching times. The very means of communication that the world uses for perversity, profanity, and to persecute the people of God will someday be used to proclaim the King. This includes not only the current and future avenues of communication, but also the people through whom it is communicated—namely you and me and all those who have yet to enter the Kingdom.

Samaria is no different from your campus or your community, and city transformation is not out of reach for the Kingdom. As you preach, go in confidence knowing that the Kingdom of God has come and is fully loaded.

Endnotes

1. Ron Steele, *Plundering Hell to Populate Heaven* (Laguna Hills, CA: Reinhard Bonnke Ministries, 1987), 80-82.

2. John Mason, *Know Your Limits, Then Ignore Them* (Insight Publishing Group: Tulsa, OK, 1999), 16.

3. F.F. Bruce, http://www.shades.org/336550.ihtml.

4. D. Thomas Lancaster, *The Mystery of the Gospel* (Littleton, CO: First Fruits Of Zion, 2003), 197.

CHAPTER 8

THE KINGDOM OF LEAVEN

"The Kingdom of Heaven is like leaven..."
(Matthew 13:33)

K INGDOM living equips us to earn a black belt in one of the most necessary skills to being an effective disciple of Christ—living in the world without living like it. This is more useful than perfecting our golf swing or developing a three-point shot. The person who can master the art of living righteously without being self-righteous has truly accomplished a great feat.

Have you ever been confused about what your attitude should be toward the world? Isaiah calls us to come out of the world while Jesus commissions us to go into all the world (see Is. 52:11; Matt. 28:19). James says friendship with the world is hatred toward God, yet Jesus was called the friend of sinners and whores (see James 4:4; Matt. 11:19). What are we supposed to do? Come out or go in? Be a friend or not?

Martin Luther once quipped, "God's truth is like a drunk trying to ride a horse. Prop him up on one side and he topples over the other." Staying centered in truth can be a precarious tightrope walk. How do we live radically without losing our relevancy? How do we live in the world as believers without becoming worldly believers? The answer is found in the life of Christ.

Change Agent

There is something about Jesus that makes people want to follow Him. Prostitutes and politicians alike became His disciples. Tax collectors, sinners, thieves, scholars, doctors, fishermen, the educated, the simple, the popular, the outcast, the young, the old, the wealthy, the destitute, men, women, and children all followed Him. Why?

Jesus is the most exciting, joyful, fun-loving, genuine, humble, transparent, and literally down-to-earth person in the universe. He was sinless yet surrounded by sin, perfect while keeping company with imperfection, fully God yet clothed in humanity. He learned the secret of being in the world but not being of it.

Jesus remained untainted because He is an influencer. When the sick get around Him, nobody walks away with the sniffles. His freedom is stronger than the bondage of the addicted and mightier than the chains of the afflicted. When Jesus shows up, the proud are humbled, the condemned are acquitted, the broken are restored, the storms are calmed, the dead are raised, and the city is changed. He once turned bathwater into fine wine. He spread an all-you-can-eat sushi bar in the desert from a little boy's sack lunch. He invented barefoot water skiing when He skated out to his disciples in the middle of the lake without a boat. He transformed Paul from a murderer to a martyr and Peter from a reed to a rock.

Jesus is not affected nor changed by His environment. Instead, he sets the atmosphere. He is the ultimate change agent, and His Kingdom is just like Him—a change agent in the world. Those who seize the Kingdom possess His influential Spirit.

The Yeast of These

Jesus likened the Kingdom of Heaven to leaven which a woman took and hid in three measures of meal until it was all leavened (see Matt. 13:33). Leavening is a process by which an agent is added to dough or batter to cause it to foam and boil up. The agent reacts with heat and moisture, trapping gas bubbles throughout the dough. When the batter is warmed, the holes left by the bubbles give the bread a soft, spongy texture.

The Greeks were avid bakers, and they sought to refine flour by eliminating its impurities. Leaven has the unique ability to assimilate to its environment and change its properties. Breads made without leaven tend to be quite heavy and compressed.

Most leavened breads are made using yeast, which is a microscopic organism that aids the fermentation process by feeding off the carbohydrates found in flour. A baker will usually set aside a small "starter" piece of old dough that can be added to new batches. Given time, the cake rises as the yeast multiplies.[1]

The Kingdom of Heaven is like leaven in this way: Though small, it has the ability to permeate all of society, causing it to boil over and rise to the occasion. It is an agent of change, altering the properties of its environment and leaving it softened toward God. The Kingdom lightens the heavy load of life's entanglements and eases the pressures of life. It eliminates impurity by refining the heart and pervading the earth with righteousness and truth.

You and I are Heaven's starter piece mixed in with the world, and over time the influence of the Kingdom will only multiply, not diminish. Someone once speculated that every person will influence at least 10,000 people in their lifetime. We could debate the credibility of this supposition, arguing the number should be smaller or perhaps bigger. Regardless, everything we do creates an investment somewhere—our relationships, our parenting, our choices, our words, our time, and our resources. Whether the investment creates a dividend or a loss depends on us. As John Gardner said, "Our lives are either sand dunes or sculptures. We are either shaped by influences or purposes."

The agents of God's Kingdom are not thermometers who merely read the temperature. We are thermostats who set the climate. We are trendsetters, and I have to continually ask myself, "Am I reporting on the climate or determining it? Am I influencing the office, the locker room, the classroom, the in-crowd, or am I allowing them to influence me?"

The Bigger Power of the Small

Jesus also likened the Kingdom to a mustard seed which a man took and sowed in his field. Though a very small seed, it grew into a large tree where birds built nests in its branches (see Matt. 13:31-32).

Here Jesus illustrates the hidden power of the small to influence the big. Like a seed planted in the soil, the Kingdom is not one to shrink but to expand. It supernaturally spreads by producing and reproducing after its own kind (see Matt. 21:43). Just as the purpose of leaven is to cause the dough to rise, the seeds of the Kingdom grow and multiply.

Like a comic book superhero, you are designed to rise to the occasion. You will mount up with wings like an eagle and cause others to soar with you. Though your life may seem insignificant now, it won't be for long, for you will spread out and produce fruit. You will live and grow to provide others with safety and shelter.

These parables also warn of a potential danger to the Kingdom. In the same manner that we can influence the world, the world can also influence us. Leaven is often symbolic for evil doctrine in Scripture, and birds can represent demonic spirits.[2] Jesus might very well be warning us against the evil influences of the world through these stories. Sin can spread like a cancer if we allow it in our mix, resulting in a monster of a bush that is a haven for demons. All the more reason we should strive to be influencers so that we don't become the influenced.

It is interesting that both seeds and leaven do not rise immediately. There is a measure of time before their effects can be appreciated. The same is true for us. Influences, both good and evil, usually won't appear overnight but given time will be obvious. They are hidden for a time as they prepare to invade its environment. Do not stop planting or kneading just because you do not see immediate results. Your prayers today will be reaped tomorrow. As surely as dough rises and as plants grow, you will make a difference in this world.

Jesus identified our influential nature when He said:

You are the salt of the earth; but if the salt loses its flavor, how shall it be seasoned? It is then good for nothing but to be thrown out and trampled underfoot by men. You are the light of the world. A city that is set on a hill cannot be hidden. Nor do they light a lamp and put it under a basket, but on a lamp- stand, and it gives light to all who are in the house. Let your light so shine before men, that they may see your good works and glorify your Father in Heaven (Matthew 5:13-16).

Salt and light are powerful instruments of influence. Salt can enhance a meal or ruin it. Light can enable us to see or blind us. Jesus cautions us to avoid two common extremes: losing our flavor and hiding our light.

Losing Our Flavor

According to Jesus, a carnal believer is like flavorless salt—good for nothing but to be discarded. Conformity neutralizes our distinction as salt of the earth. If we are living like the rest of the world, why would they come to us for guidance? If we are bumpin' to the same music, vulgar in our words, and spending our time and money as the world does, they will not look to us for spiritual help.

While the believer who gets high and gambles with his unbelieving buddies may have a mission field of friends, he will have no message of power to give them. If we are indistinguishable from the world, we may have an audience, but we will have no message. The depressed, the alco- holic, the drug dealer, or the playboy wanting out of their destructive lifestyle will not grab a lifeline from this kind of believer.

Are you a salt substitute? What do you taste like to Christ and to your world? There is an old proverb that says: "A ship in the sea is all right, but the sea in the ship is all wrong." We can take this to mean that the Kingdom in the world is all right, but the world in the Kingdom is all wrong. Let's keep the world out of the Kingdom by keeping it out of our hearts, minds, homes, and behavior.

A good place to start is our homes. Do an inventory check of the music, movies, books, and magazines in your house, and ask the Holy Spirit to show you what material offends Him. Then, simply remove it.

I try to do these Holy Ghost check-ups periodically. Recently, He highlighted some movies that were in our cabinet that contained some sexual humor. Though we are very particular with our entertainment and what we allow our kids to watch, it was not humor appropriate for children. The Lord instructed me that just as I seek to protect my children's innocence, so I should with my own spirit. If it is inappropriate for my son and daughter, why would it be appropriate for my spirit? I imagine the Holy Spirit doesn't enjoy watching those scenes through my eyes. Needless to say, the movies are gone.

Hiding Our Light

Jesus also cautions us against hiding our light. It appears that our tendency to create cliques and become spiritual separatists is not unique to the western church. The danger here is that, while the segregated church may be sanctified, it builds no bridge for evangelism. Isolation continues to be a constant barrier to modern-day evangelism. A monk confined to a monastery may have pure thoughts and a burning passion to preach, but he will have no audience with which to share his revelations if he remains a recluse.

> *I do not pray that You should take them out of the world, but that You should keep them from the evil one. They are not of the world, just as I am not of the world. Sanctify them by Your truth. Your word is truth. As You sent Me into the world, I also have sent them into the world* (John 17:15-18).

Are you artificial lighting? Does your light only shine when others turn theirs on? Some believers are so afraid of contamination by worldliness that they are afraid of any social contact with the world. Separation to God is not demonstrated by separating from the associations of the world but rather in personal lifestyle. We are to be spiritually distinct, not socially segregated.

I wrote to you in my epistle not to keep company with sexually immoral people. Yet I certainly did not mean with the sexually immoral people of this world, or with the covetous, or extortioners, or idolaters, since then you would need to go out of the world. But now I have written to you not to keep company with anyone named a brother, who is sexually immoral, or covetous, or an idolater, or a reviler, or a drunkard, or an extortioner—not even to eat with such a person. For what have I to do with judging those also who are outside? Do you not judge those who are inside? But those who are outside God judges. Therefore put away from yourselves the evil person (1 Corinthians 5:9-13).

Like a mustard seed, there is a measure of growth that cannot be achieved unless we are planted in the soils of the world. Pressure and resistance have a way of forming diamonds and muscles, and God is the mama bird kicking us out of the nest, forcing us to fly. His Kingdom is designed to be planted in the center of society so that His influence can increase as we do.

On the Rise

My Dad used to take my brother and me shark fishing in the San Francisco Bay. We had only a 17-foot ski boat, so we stayed mostly in the shallow parts of the Bay, but what great fun it was. We used squid for bait and a hook with a leader line, and we caught scores of small sand and leopard sharks. Once time we caught a pregnant shark and brought home a few newborn baby sharks for our aquarium. They were so cute. They survived the ride home, but unfortunately they couldn't survive the suction of the aquarium filter.

Most fish adapt to their environment. I am told that if you were to confine one of those baby sharks, it would remain a size proportionate to the aquarium in which it lives. It can be six inches long but fully mature. But the day it is released into the ocean, the shark will resume growing to normal size.

The day of your release has come. For us to retreat from the world now and deprive it of light will only stunt our growth and rob God of receiving glory. Satan is well aware of this fact. If he cannot get us involved in the affairs of the world, he will bully us out of the world. But you belong to a Kingdom of people that will not tolerate this.

Influencers permeate their environment in five ways:

1. Effect. Effect means "the ability to bring about results." Something that is effective makes an impression on the mind of its observer. The Kingdom effectively impacts whatever it comes into contact with. It has the ability to make a lasting impression on people.

> *Let no one despise your youth, but be an example to the believers in word, in conduct, in love, in spirit, in faith, in purity* (1 Timothy 4:12).

The Greek word for "example" is *tupos.* It means "an imprint, impression, the mark of a blow, or a pattern to be imitated." The word is also translated "mold, dye, stamp, or scar."[3] In other words, Paul instructs Timothy to tattoo his world through godly speech, action, love, faithfulness, and integrity.

2. Affect. The Kingdom of leaven is like spiritual caffeine to a sluggish world. It rouses change and requires a response. Affect means "to be a stimulant or to move someone to a response."[4] Just because a church purchases property in a city does not automatically assure that it is now salt and light to its community. Only when the glory of God is actively rising in the midst of God's people will the Kingdom of leaven spread.

3. Defect. Kingdom living empowers us to go against the grain and swim upstream. In the military, defectors are soldiers who rebel against their commanding officer, forsake their comrades, abandon the army, and join ranks with the opposition. In the same way, we are now defectors of a world-system, rebelling against the majority, breaking ranks with the devil, forsaking our past behavioral patterns, and joining the cause of the transcendent.

A few years back, Carolyn Risher served as the mayor of Inglis, a small fishing community in Florida. Inspired by the events of September 11, 2001, she issued a decree banning satan from town. When asked by a reporter, "Does satan live in Inglis?" her response was, "Satan lives where we let him."[5] The devil will make his home wherever he desires, even in our minds if we let him. As Kingdom loyalists, let's make this same declaration of independence from the devil as Carolyn did.

4. Infect. Paul was infectious. Standing before Felix, the lawyer Tertullus accused the apostle of being a cult leader. Mounting a case against him, he added, "*For we have found this man to be a plague*" (Acts 24:5). Tertullus was comparing Paul to a bad virus, and I imagine Paul was grinning from ear to ear. The lawyer didn't realize he had paid this apostle a very fine compliment.

Paul was a walking epidemic and a pathological lover of God. Whatever he did, he was contagious. Wherever he went, people caught his fire. Could it be that we would be as influential as he was? That our faith would be as contagious and infectious as a virus? Plagues are communicable. They only spread by contact. Paul understood that he could communicate without contamination, but he could not communicate without contact.

I have a friend named Guido who came to Christ while studying engineering at Chico State University. Before his conversion, Guido was climbing telephone poles inciting drunken collegians to bounce police cars and riot during Rancho Chico Days. After his conversion, God used that passion to fashion him into a witnessing machine.

Once, he and some friends were getting frozen yogurt at the local favorite Jon and Bon's yogurt shop near campus. He was so burdened for college students that he couldn't contain himself. He used a nearby garbage can for a stage and began to preach Christ to the patrons as they ate frozen yogurt. Today Guido is a minister, but it was his boldness that day that influenced two people to come into the Kingdom.

The word *influenza* comes from the word *influence*, and the Kingdom of God is like the flu; it is infectious and transferable. It is a holy outbreak that has come to break people out of bondage. It is a righteous disease meant to "dis-ease" some devils and plague the kingdom of darkness. Like pestilence, it isn't satisfied until everyone is infected. Anthrax,

SARS, E. coli, Ebola, West Nile Virus, bird flus, and swine flus are nothing compared to the threat of this glorious Kingdom.

5. Reflect. Have you ever noticed that Jesus had no sooner proclaimed, "I am the light of the world," than He pointed to his followers and declared, "*You are the light of the world*" (John 9:5; Matt. 5:14)? This indicates that our identity in the earth is a reflection of Christ's glory. First John 4:17 says, "*...as He is, so are we in this world.*" John reveals that what we *are* in this world is what Christ *is* in Heaven.

Conclusion

> *Do not be drunk on wine...but be filled with the Spirit* (Ephesians 5:18).

Luther was right. Being drunk on wine causes one to topple over into dangerous areas of imbalance and compromise. However, the disciples left the upper room drunk in a different manner—drunk in the Spirit—and it caused them to spill their influence out onto the streets. Living under the influence of the King is a holy intoxication, a heavenly inebriation. Only when we are under the influence *of* God can we really be an influence *for* Him.

You are a holy vessel living in an unholy culture, and the Kingdom of leaven is on the rise through you. When you mix the yeast of the Kingdom with your faith, the Kingdom will advance in your life, in your home, and in your community. Be encouraged to know that the spirit of influence that rested on Christ not only rests on you, but can rest on your family, your church, your city, and your nation.

Endnotes

1. Microsoft Encarta Encyclopedia, computer software, version Deluxe 2000 (Microsoft Corporation, 1999).

2. Kevin Conner, *Interpreting The Symbols and Types* (Portland, OR: City Bible Publishing, 1980), 130, 152.

3. Spiros Zodhiates, *The Complete Wordstudy New Testament* (Chattanooga, TN: AMG Publishers, 1992), 941; Francis Brown, S. Driver, and C. Briggs, *BibleSoft's Brown, Driver and Briggs' Hebrew Lexicon* (Ontario, Canada: Woodside Bible Fellowship, 1993); James Strong, *BibleSoft's New Exhaustive Strong's Numbers and Concordance with Expanded Greek-Hebrew Dictionary* (Nashville, TN: Thomas Nelson Inc., 1994).

4. *Webster's New World Dictionary*, s.v. "Affect."

5. Gary Tuchman, "Florida town casts out Satan," *CNN.com*, January 29, 2002, http://archives.cnn.com/2002/US/01/29/town.satan/ (accessed March 31, 2009).

CHAPTER 9

UNLEASHING HEAVEN ON EARTH

"They will come from the east and the west, from the north and the south, and sit down in the kingdom of God."
(Luke 13:29)

HEAVEN is not your stomping grounds. If it were, you would have been born an angel instead of a human. As disappointing as it may sound, *earth* is your domain (see Ps. 115:16). While I'm sure you wouldn't object to visiting the third heaven on occasion as Paul did, your physical body is designed to live and walk on planet earth. This is evidenced by the fact that you are still living in the land of the breathing. When we mistakenly make getting to Heaven our lone spiritual quest, we set ourselves up for grave disappointment and a sincerely misguided life.

However, this does not mean we are confined to just earthly things, for we sit together in heavenly places in Christ (see Eph. 2:6). Paul admonishes us to set our minds on things above, not on the things of the earth (see Col. 3:2). When our mindset is limited to the things of the earth, we lose touch with reality—the reality of Heaven.

Peter made this mistake. Right after Jesus hands him the keys to the Kingdom, Peter rebukes Christ as He foretells of His imminent death and resurrection. The Lord then turns and says to Peter, "*Get behind me, satan! You are an offense to Me, for you are not mindful of the things of God, but the things of men*" (Matt. 16:23).

Jesus was calling the devil out—out of Peter's mindset. There is something satanic about a mind full of earthly thoughts. James describes these thoughts as earthly, sensual, and even demonic (see James 3:15). It is an offense to Christ when we allow our calculation to interfere with His revelation, and when we utter these thoughts from our lips it actually gives place to the devil.

Some people have been accused of being too heavenly-minded to be of any earthly good, but I wonder if the people who say this really know what is on Heaven's mind. I have quickly realized that my problem is not that I am too heavenly-minded to be of earthly good. More often I am too earthly-minded to be of any heavenly good! I have missed countless divine appointments and opportunities to bless someone else, because I was too busy thinking about what I needed to buy at the store or what I wanted for lunch.

Divine Fusion

When God created you He had more in mind for you than just securing your name in the Book of Life. Although we rejoice in this glorious truth, you and I are not citizens of earth trying to get to Heaven (see Luke 10:20). We are citizens of Heaven living on the earth. We are to set our minds on Heaven and our feet on earth. Our aim is both Heaven and earth, literally Heaven *on* earth!

Adam was originally made of spirit and dust—a synthesis of Heaven and earth. Now One greater than him has come. This Last Adam was fully God and fully man, a divine fusion of spirit and matter. Because we are found in Him, our inheritance is also a mixture of Heaven and earth. We get the privilege of tasting the best of both worlds, and this union of divinity and humanity can only be reclaimed through the Kingdom.

Uncommon Prayers

Kingdom living not only changes the way we think; it also changes the way we pray. When we set our minds on things above, our prayers become more Kingdom minded and less common.

Common prayers say: *I want more of God.* Kingdom prayers say: *God, here is more of me.*

Common prayers say: *I need humility.* Kingdom prayers say: *I humble myself.*

Common prayers say: *I want to be popular.* Kingdom prayers say: *I want to be popular in Heaven.*

Common prayers say: *Help me resist temptation.* Kingdom prayers say: *Help me avoid temptation.*

Common prayers say: *Lord, I want my blessing.* Kingdom prayers say: *Lord, bless others as I bless You.*

Common prayers say: *Give me riches.* Kingdom prayers say: *Give me poor people that I can be rich toward.*

Common prayers say: *Deliver me.* Kingdom prayers say: *Deliver others as I glorify You through my deliverance.*

Common prayers say: *Save me.* Kingdom prayers say: *Save my enemy.*

As It Is in Heaven

Jesus prayed an uncommon prayer when He prayed:

> *Our Father in Heaven, hallowed be Your name. Your Kingdom come. Your will be done on earth as it is in Heaven. Give us this day our daily bread. And forgive us our debts, as we forgive our debtors. And do not lead us into temptation, but deliver us from the evil one. For Yours is the kingdom and the power and the glory forever. Amen (Matthew 6:8-13).*

The Kingdom is mentioned twice in this 66-word prayer, and at the heart of the Lord's Prayer we find the express purpose of Christ. It is to bring Heaven to us. He desires that the atmosphere of Heaven reign over the atmosphere of the earth, and we would be hard pressed to find a better definition of the will of God than this.

Here is a general rule of thumb when it comes to the will of God. If it exists in Heaven, it is to exist on earth. Likewise, if it doesn't exist in Heaven, it is safe to assume that it is not God's will. For example, truth, purity, peace, and laughter are to fill the earth just as they fill Heaven. Conversely, bigotry, pornography, rape, murder, and every other shameful thing should be banished from the planet, because they have no place in Heaven. Earth is to be Heaven's echo, and just as the image of Christ reflects the image of the Father, so the inhabitants of earth are to reflect Heaven. We are designed to be Heaven's mirror.

People wonder, "Is it God's will that I am sick?" The answer is simple. Will there be disease and pain in Heaven? Of course not, and if there were it would not be Heaven! The Kingdom of Heaven is exactly that—heavenly. Sickness was not a reality for Adam and Eve until they got banned from the Garden, and neither is it the will of God for those in the Kingdom. Through Christ, Eden's benefit package has become ours.

Third Heaven Invasion

The operation of Heaven on earth is a great mystery. When Jesus prayed, "Your Kingdom come," He was not just referencing the existing Kingdom but the emerging Kingdom as well. It is a dual prophetic prayer entreating Heaven to come now and to come then. When we grab hold of the spirit of this prayer, God will bring us a visitation that prepares a generation for a habitation.

There is a fascinating account written about Chinese orphans who experienced a profound visitation of Heaven. It happened in Uuuanfu, China, in the early 1920s at the Adullam Rescue Mission. The story tells of street kids who were caught up to Heaven in the spirit on multiple occasions. There they described playing harps, seeing Jesus, talking with angels, eating heavenly fruit, speaking in another language, walking the streets of the Golden City, foreseeing future events, and standing before God's throne. They described Heaven as a place with singing birds, leaping dear, friendly lions, blooming flowers, golden trees, indescribable beauty, and overwhelming joy.

Jesus loves children, especially orphans. What is so telling about this story is that these revelations were not given to the adults but to the children. These were not the royal class of society nor were they scholars. They were poor, uneducated boys ranging from age 6 to 18. They were rejects who grew up begging for food and stealing for survival, but came to know Christ through the outreach of this mission. They had no formal biblical training yet they accurately and harmoniously described specific details of Heaven found only in Scripture. God gave these unexpecting and underprivileged orphans one of the most unprecedented glimpses of His own backyard.[1]

John had visions of his own and describes seeing an ancient tree in his apocalyptic vision. The Tree of Life suddenly reemerges on the scene after making a disappearance after the Fall. This life-giving tree must be special because fallen humanity was banished from the Garden because of its presence (see Gen. 3:23-24). Because the Tree of Life is found at the beginning and end of biblical history, it indicates that the Kingdom of God commences and culminates in Edenic fashion. After Adam, the world drastically spun away from perfection, but God is bringing the earth back to its original design through the Last Adam. When we enter the Kingdom, we participate in the coming age of restoration, which is the earth returning to a state of perfection under the sovereign rule of God. The redeemed of the Kingdom now obtain what Adam and Eve had lost—access to eternal life.

Eden reveals that Heaven and earth are meant to be divinely connected, and prayer is the principal agent used to achieve this end. This is where you and I come into the picture. God is establishing His invisible Kingdom in the visible world, and we have been appointed as administrators of His estate. Our mission is not to get people to Heaven, but to bring Heaven to them.

But how do we accomplish this? Here are some ways:

1. Surrender to the mission.

> *Therefore submit to God. Resist the devil and he will flee from you* (James 4:7).

In order to release Heaven on earth, we must know what God wants to do. Submitting to God keeps us current with Him. When we don't know His voice or His Word, we tend to do the opposite of what we should. Instead of submitting to God and resisting the devil we find ourselves submitting to the devil and resisting God! Unfortunately, I've made this error all too often. Surrender to God keeps us from being ignorant of the will of God.

Submission means to come under a mission. Spiritually, it implies that we bring the mission of our lives under the mission of Christ. Once we learn "sub-mission," He awards us "co-mission," the Great Commission. In other words, we get to work alongside the Holy Spirit in the mission. When we are faithful with commission, the Father then grants us per-mission. This means we can spend this, do that, and go there as long as it has something to do with the mission.

When Meljoné and I were looking into buying a home, I asked the Lord if He was releasing us to be homeowners. He replied, "Will you use it for the Kingdom?" A few months later on the night we moved in, we consecrated our new home to the Lord and to the Kingdom. We anointed every wall with oil and made Scriptural declarations at the four corners of the property. We try now to live with an understanding that our house is not just for our enjoyment, but also to benefit the Kingdom of God.

2. Raise the level of your experience to match the Word of God.

Jesus prayed for God's will to be accomplished on earth for one obvious reason: Not everything that happens on earth is the will of God. The Kingdom of Heaven offers a solution to this. Just because there is terrible injustice in the world or something horrific has happened to you does not mean that God willed it. Our tendency is to lower the standard of God's Word to match the current level of our experience, but instead we should raise the level of our current experience to meet the standard of God's Word. The will of God is not mechanical, so let's contend for nothing short of total victory.

3. Pay attention to the activities of Heaven.

> ...*Most assuredly, I say to you, the Son can do nothing of Himself, but what He sees the Father do; for whatever He does, the Son also does in like manner* (John 5:19).

Ask the Father to show you what He is doing. Bringing Heaven to earth necessitates that we ascertain the will of God and campaign for it on earth. If we see God up to something, then we have the backing of Heaven to dive into that pursuit. Attempting to do something that the Father is not doing will only prove to be fruitless. Ask for heavenly eyesight that yields divine insight.

4. Declare the will of God.

I am told that the verb tense of "Your Kingdom come, Your will be done" is not so much a request as it is a command. It literally renders, "Kingdom, *come!* Will, *be done!*" It suggests that releasing Heaven on earth demands more than just a petition; it requires a declaration.

Don't confess what you see in the natural. Confess what you see in the spirit. If you are praying for your child to come to Christ or for a relationship to be restored, don't declare what has been the pattern. Declare what will be. Through your words, you can transport the will of God from the invisible to the visible.

I have made it a practice to make spiritual declarations over my family as we sit down to enjoy the Sabbath meal. As priest of my home, my words have the ability to generate blessings or curses. The Lord instructed Aaron and his sons to speak a blessing over the children of Israel, and each night I like to declare it over my children before they go to bed. You can try it too if you like.

> *The Lord bless you and keep you;*
> *The Lord make His face to shine upon you,*

And be gracious to you;
The Lord lift up His countenance upon you,
And give you peace (Numbers 6:24-26).

5. Invest in Heaven's thoughts.

The world that we give our attention to the most is the world that has the most influence over us. The more consideration we give to wicked things, the more influence darkness has over us. The more mindful we are of Heaven's activities, the more victoriously we live here on earth. When we invest our energies in Heaven, we reap its benefits on earth.

6. Stay in hot pursuit.

God is sovereign. He can do whatever He desires. Yet at the same time He has revealed His character to us so that we are not left ignorant about what He requires. Jesus Christ is the living Word of God. Through His life and ministry we come to understand what God truly wants. Time spent at the feet the Master is never wasted. With every encounter we better understand what He wants us to accept, reject, and pray.

7. What you seek is what you get.

Have you ever noticed that you don't have to go looking for problems? Problems have a way of finding you. The Kingdom of Heaven is not like this. It does not stalk us. In order to find the Kingdom it must be sought after. Jesus highlighted this when He said, "*Seek first the Kingdom of God and His righteousness, and all these things shall be added unto you*" (Matt. 6:33).

You have heard of the phrase, "What you see is what you get." Here is a profound Kingdom principle: "What you *seek* is what you get!" This truth works in the Kingdom as it does in life. If we seek trouble, trouble will find us. If we seek money, wealth will come our way. If we look to cheat or steal, suddenly our eyes will be opened to these opportunities. But if we seek the things of Heaven, our Father will not give us a stone, serpent, or scorpion. He will give us heavenly things (see Matt. 7:7-11; Luke 11:9-13).

He who earnestly seeks good finds favor, but trouble will come
to him who seeks evil (Proverbs 11:27).

Christ promises that if we seek first the Kingdom, along the path we will find everything we need for the journey. This means that Heaven does not automatically fall into our laps. It requires a stalker.

The first time I witnessed someone operate in a word of knowledge, I was floored. God accomplished in twenty seconds what twenty years of counseling could not. I was deeply moved. The exposure I received to the work of the Spirit that day placed a hunger in me for the revelatory gifts. That hunger then led to prayer, which in turn led to faith and the operation of that gift in my ministry.

Paul said to *"eagerly desire spiritual gifts, especially the gift of prophecy"* (1 Cor. 14:1 NIV). Spiritual gifts are love empowered. It is right to desire them, but they are not involuntary. They require cooperation on our part with God.

Whatever kingdom we give preeminence to we will inherit. If we give priority to the Kingdom of Heaven we will reap its benefits, and from the Kingdom we sow into today we will reap tomorrow. In eternity, every person inherits the kingdom he or she served. If we live only for ourselves we will find ourselves on the wrong side of eternity, but when we make God's Kingdom our first priority, He guarantees that our concerns will be His concerns. Like Jesus, when we take care of our Father's business, He will take care of ours. That's a pretty good deal.

Inheriting the Earth

...it is your Father's good pleasure to give you the kingdom
(Luke 12:32).

We are not just coming into the Kingdom; we are becoming a kingdom, and this kingdom is not only our vocation; it is our inheritance. What we are doing now is linked to what we are coming into. Like a master stockbroker, the Father has invested our futures in the Kingdom of Heaven. We are now beneficiaries of God's estate and co-heirs with Christ.

Scripture is clear that there is an eternal inheritance laid up for the righteous (see Acts 20:32; 26:18; 1 Cor. 1:9; 15:50; Gal. 5:21; Eph. 5:5; Col. 1:12; 3:24; Heb. 1:14; 6:12; 9:15; 1 Peter 1:4; and Rev. 21:7). This means that your devotion to Christ is not in vain. It is reaping lasting rewards for you, others, and the Kingdom. It also means that your inheritance in God's Kingdom is both present and approaching.

Possessing the earth is part of our inheritance. David wrote, "...*those who wait on the Lord, they shall inherit the earth*" (Psalm 37:9). Jesus said, "*Blessed are the meek, for they shall inherit the earth*" (Matt. 5:5). The saints of God are poised to possess the very soil we walk on. This means we should maintain a positive outlook about the earth, for no one has been given a greater hope and promise for the future of the earth than the saints of God.

Conclusion

According to Scripture, those who possess the Kingdom will eventually take over the earth, and the New Jerusalem will be the capital city of the Kingdom. This heavenly city is the church, the Bride of Christ. Jesus is the very foundation of the city of God, whose builder and maker is God, and the Father will dwell with humankind forever. Augustine once said of the New Jerusalem, "Who would not yearn for that city out of which no friend departs, into which no enemy enters."[2]

I am confident that you will be a citizen of that holy city. You will be in Heaven. Just know that Heaven will be setting up camp here on earth.

Endnotes

1. H.A. Baker, *Visions Beyond the Veil*, Public Domain.

2. BibleSoft's *Jamison, Fausset and Brown Commentary*. Electronic Database (Seattle, WA: Biblesoft, 1997).

CHAPTER 10

THE REAL WORLD

"Find out what happens when people stop being polite and start getting real."
—Advertisement for MTV's reality show The Real World

W E live in an age of fakes, phonies, and virtual realities. We advertise facial makeovers, plastic surgeries, collagen implants, and body enhancements. We eat processed cheese, imitation vanilla, egg substitutes, and artificial crab. We manufacture fake diamonds, produce staged entertainment, and even have spray-on hair. We don't just like sports. We like to play them in the world of make-believe.

The lines between what is real and what is virtually real are becoming less defined. Paul spoke of this trend, saying, *"Creation fell into subjection to failure and unreality"* (Rom. 8:20 Weymouth New Testament). But there is a higher reality than the fantasy football variety. It is a tangible hope, a genuine adventure. It is a real world, one that is perceptible yet hidden. It is God's reality, and when we get into God's world His reality becomes ours.

According to A.W. Tozer, reality is "that which has existence apart from any idea any mind can have of it and which would exist if there were no mind anywhere to entertain a thought of it. That which is real has being in itself. It does not depend on the observer for its validity."[1]

According to this definition, reality is God. He is the most real Being in the universe.

The Kingdom is real in every sense of the word. It exists because God exists and is eternal because God is eternal. If people never conceive, consume, or comprehend the Kingdom, it is still real, and it does not require a laboratory, library, or lobotomy to confirm its existence.

Superior Reality

Society is intrigued by the spiritual dimension. Hollywood writes screenplays about it. Authors tell stories. Reporters write blogs. They use nebulous terms like paranormal, mystical, ghosts, apparitions, warm spots, goose bumps, chi, and energy to describe it. Yet there is nothing more tangible than the spiritual realm.

Contrary to our material perspective, the spiritual is not a shadow of the physical. Rather, we are a shadow of the unseen. The invisible created the visible, so the unseen world must have come into being before the natural world did. "*In the beginning, God created the heavens and the earth*" (Gen. 1:1). What we see with our eyes today exists only because the spiritual world does. All that we can see, hear, taste, smell, and feel is a created temporary, a consequence of a hidden reality.

It is not that the physical is imaginary. Your pain, your setback, and your headache are real enough, especially to you. It is just that the spiritual world is a superior reality. It has the ability to affect and alter our current reality. It is a higher, even stronger reality.

What if our eyes were suddenly opened to the spiritual dimension? What would we see? Angels? Demons? God? I am confident we would be more spiritual by default. We would view life as more ordered by spiritual forces than previously assumed. I have no doubt we would live differently, and this is what the reality of the Kingdom is designed to do—completely alter our perspective and application of life.

Spiritual Beings

You are not just an assortment of arteries and amino acids, chemicals and cholesterol, serotonin and cilia, enzymes and epidermis, muscles and mitochondria. You are a spiritual being navigating your way through a material world. Our bodies are made from a product of earth and will eventually return to being dust. This explains why we receive a new, spiritual body at the resurrection. But when God created our innermost being, He used His own eternal material, a product of Heaven. This product is called spirit, and our spirits live on even when our earthly bodies don't.

A spiritual body behaves differently than a physical body. After His resurrection, Jesus' spiritual body did what any physical body could do. He ate, spoke with, and was touched by the disciples (see Luke 24:36-43). Yet He was also able to do what physical bodies cannot do. He flew, appeared, disappeared, and defied the laws of science. Jesus demonstrated this to the disciples in the upper room. Though the doors were shut, Jesus suddenly appeared in their midst (see John 20:19,26). The Bible does not elaborate, but He must have either walked through a closed door or spontaneously materialized right before them. We tend to think that the Lord's resurrected body must have been vaporous like a ghost, but then how could Thomas have put His hand in His side if Jesus was merely a phantom? The opposite is more likely. Jesus is extra-dimensional, and if it is true that He can walk through walls, the wall would be ghostlike compared to His molecularly-dense body. Our Lord is literally more real than matter.

The Substance of Spirit

Spirit is not like matter. Matter can be observed through the physical senses. You can pinch it, poke it, pull it, prod it, pick it up, and bounce it around. Matter is pebbles, leaves, skin, water, and dust. It possesses weight, has size, and takes up space.

Spirit, however, is an altogether different kind of substance. It doesn't necessarily have weight, dimension, size, or shape. Jesus said, "*The words that I speak to you are spirit, and they are life"* (John 6:63). He didn't say His words were *full of* spirit, but rather they *are* spirit. So we see that spirit is less measurable yet far superior to matter. Spirit controls matter. This means that a person who is Spirit-filled has authority over matter.

I once read about a believer who was aboard an airplane when it experienced a horrible malfunction in the air that led to several lives being lost. It happened in 1989. United Airlines flight 811 was on a scheduled flight from Honolulu to Sydney. Only a few minutes after takeoff, a cargo door ripped off the side of the plane. It left a gaping hole in the aircraft and sucked nine people to their deaths over the Pacific Ocean. It was a tragic accident, but what the newspapers didn't report was that a Spirit-filled believer was occupying the seat right next to the blown-out section of the airplane.

A few minutes before the incident, he describes hearing an inner voice tell him to get up from his seat and move to another one. At first he brushed it off, but he testifies that he heard the voice tell him again more emphatically to move. Recognizing the leading of the Spirit, he promptly moved and his life was spared. It was only seconds later that the door ripped open.

Entering the real world of the Kingdom can save your life and the lives of others. Learning to navigate through it opens us up to countless possibilities, but this kind of leading does not come to the casual observer. It only comes to the true seeker of the Kingdom.

How can God's real world become our reality?

1. Faith unlocks the experience.

Our faith should move us beyond pious creeds and straight into zealous deeds. Biology teaches that something is real if it can be proved through the scientific method. It says we must experience something before we can believe it. But Jesus teaches the opposite. He says we first believe in order to experience. He is advocating experiential faith.

> *Enoch walked with God, and he was not, for God took him* (Genesis 5:24).

Enoch lived an intriguing life. Given only a few obscure verses in the book of Genesis, he is described as a man who walked with God for three hundred years. The grandfather of Noah, Enoch encountered God so profoundly that at the age of 365 he disappeared off the face of the planet. Enoch must have been more at home in Heaven than he was on earth.

I heard a story about a little girl who was telling her mother what she learned in church. She said, "Mom, we learned about a man named Enoch. He used to go for long walks with God. One day they walked so far and so long, God said to Enoch, 'You are too far from home. You had better come stay at my place.'"

The writer of Hebrews says, *"By faith, Enoch was taken away so that he did not see death...before he was taken he had this testimony, that he pleased God"* (Heb. 11:5). Faith pleases God and unlocks the door to the real world. If we will take God at His word, we will stumble upon the supernatural in ways the scientist only dreams of. His "video game experience" will pale in comparison to the adventure of your Kingdom exploits. Lacking faith or having faith in the wrong things will only deadbolt the door and bar us from encountering the spiritual dimension.

In Revelation 21:8, the Lord describes the kinds of people who will inhabit hell. It is not "light" *Reader's Digest* material. The list includes liars, murderers, sorcerers, idolaters, the sexually immoral, and the corrupt, but the very first to top the list are the cowardly and unbelieving. Why is this? It is because fear negates faith. Fear and unbelief honor the natural world above the spiritual. They imprison us to the visible and anchor us to a mere natural, carnal existence. Ultimately, fear and unbelief will confine a person to a deceptive life of unreality, causing him or her to miss the reality of the Kingdom.

2. The real world is closed to the intellect.

If given too much power, the mind can become an evil dictator. Intelligence is important, but it is not primary. Kingdom exploits are accessed through the mind of the Spirit; they cannot be accessed through reason and logic alone. Our thinking must submit to our spirit, and if we want to be led by the Spirit we cannot afford to let our minds dictate our hearts.

Just because a person is intelligent does not mean that he or she is wise. Knowledge is nothing if we never act upon it, and wisdom cannot be gained through education alone. We only gain what we learn through application and action.

I firmly believe God can use a willing and open person more than He can use an overly intelligent one. Why? A person who relies too strongly on his or her intellect has to figure it all out before he or she will move, and by that time it is too late.

There have been times when God has nudged to me to witness to a stranger, but I have had too much to think about to readily obey. Full of excuses, I'm thinking to myself, "I can't right now. I have too many errands to finish. I am not sure what to say. What if they know the Bible better than me? What if I turn them away from Christ more? Wait a second. Is this really God leading me? Does God still speak anyway? Am I hearing voices? Am I going crazy?" It becomes an endless, fruitless internal battle that often results in nonaction.

But when the Holy Spirit nudges a willing vessel, he or she leaves the shopping cart, walks over, and lets the words fly. He or she is simply smart enough to believe and obey. I want to be smart like that, not allowing my intellect to interfere with God's intentions.

3. It requires blue eyes.

Have you ever bought a new car and noticed the same model practically everywhere on the road? You spot one here in a different color and there with a luggage rack. Is it that suddenly everyone buys the same vehicle at the same time as you? No. You simply have new eyes to see those cars on the road. The same is true for the Kingdom. The real world gravitates toward those who seek it out.

Do this exercise with me. Find five things in the place you are sitting that are the color blue. Did you find five things? I'll bet you didn't notice all of those blue objects around you until now. Why? You have blue eyes and a blue mindset. Be sure to put on your blue eyes before you go out in public.

One time I was at the gym talking with God as I was working out. I was asking Him to teach me how to hear His voice better when He pointed out a beautiful girl who just walked through the door. He said, "Do you see that girl?" I was thinking, "This is it. She must be my future wife!"

Knowing my thoughts, He replied, "No, but she is in a lot of turmoil." He began to tell me specifics about her life, about how her father rejected her and that she was going through a bitter divorce. Honestly, I would have never gathered any of that information by her appearance. She seemed quite happy behind that pretty smile of hers. The Lord then said, "Never use your natural eyes to determine what is happening spiritually."

"Wow," I thought. "What a great nugget from the Lord." In my excitement about this new insight, I didn't even think to pray for the girl, until the Holy Spirit told me to go over and prophesy over her. I said, "Uh, I didn't know there was going to be homework!" Honestly, I was terrified to prophesy to her. I told the Lord that if she came over and began using the machine next to me, then I knew it was a sign that I should talk to her. I was mildly shocked when she did, but nevertheless I began to share the word of the Lord with her. I could see the tears well up in her eyes as I told her about the acceptance and love of a Heavenly Father. While she did not become my wife, I hope that she is pursuing the Lover of her soul.

We always see the Kingdom better when we are looking for it. That encounter would have never happened had I not put on my blue eyes and been looking *"to see what He will say to me"* (Hab. 2:1). Paul writes, *"We do not look at the things which are seen, but at the things which are not seen. For the things which are seen are temporary, but the things which are not seen are eternal"* (2 Cor. 4:18).

The Story of Sha

I read an inspiring story about a 17-year-old girl named Laura who had been missing for eight days in Washington State. She was last seen at a party, and when she was absent the next day, her family filed a missing persons report.

A statewide bulletin was released, and search parties were assembled. For several days, friends and family retraced the route Laura most likely drove home that night. They focused on a stretch of highway coming from a neighborhood east of Washington Lake near Redmond, but with no success. After eight days, the Sheriff's department had all but written her off as a runaway, and her parents had lost hope. Her mother, Jean, said, "We had already given her up and let her be dead in our hearts."

But Sha Nohr, a family friend, had been praying for Laura and the situation. She had several vivid dreams of a wooded area and felt impressed by the Holy Spirit to jump in the car and drive. She drove the two-lane winding road, praying all the way. At each turn, the Holy Spirit would say, "Keep going. Keep going."

She felt drawn to stop in an area where 200 volunteers had unsuccessfully searched the day before. She noticed an open space between the guardrails, and as she peered over the concrete barrier it reminded her of the place in her dreams. She climbed down the steep and densely-vegetated embankment, and as she made her way down the 200-foot ravine, she spotted Laura's crumpled Toyota Camry in the trees. Laura was badly hurt and severely dehydrated, but alive and conscious in the back seat.

Laura was brought to Harborview Medical Center in Seattle, and the medical staff were astonished that she was still alive after eight days without food or water. The hospital said dehydration saved her life by preventing a blood clot from expanding in her brain, but we know who really saved her life. When word of her survival reached more than 100 people gathered for a vigil, the meeting turned into a prayer celebration with singing and thanksgiving.[2]

Conclusion

This is the real world, and these kinds of stories will not be uncommon as we approach the coming age of the kingdom. The Holy Spirit is going to employ ordinary citizens of His kingdom to appropriate the mysteries of the spirit. This real word does not come to the casual. It comes to those who are looking for the kingdom.

Endnotes

1. A.W. Tozer, *The Pursuit of God* (Wheaton, IL: Tyndale House, 1982), 52.

2. http://www.ntsb.gov/ntsb/brief.asp?ev_id=20001213X27705&key=1, (accessed May 1, 2009).

3. Natalie Singer, "Redmond teenager survives 8 days stuck in car wreck," *The Seattle Times*, October 11, 2004, http://seattletimes.nwsource.com/html/localnews/2002059533_missinggirl11m.html (accessed April 3, 2009); KOMO Staff and News Services, "Redmond Teen Survives For Days In Car At Bottom Of Ravine," *KOMOTV.com*, October 10, 2004, http://www.komonews.com/news/archive/4135481.html (accessed April 03, 2009); Jaime Holguin, "8 Days After Wreck, A Miracle Find," *CBSNews.com*, October 12, 2004, http://www.cbsnews.com/stories/2004/10/11/national/main648658.shtml (accessed April 3, 2009); "Doctors: Dehydration May Have Saved Girl," CNN.com article, October 12, 2004, AP, (accessed 10/15/2004); http://www.foxnews.com/story/0,2933,135140,00.html

SECTION 3

CONFLICT IN THE KINGDOM

"The Kingdom of Heaven suffers violence, and the violent take it by force."
(Matthew 11:12)

E VERY morning we wake up in the middle of something already in motion. The sun is shining. The earth is spinning. The clock is ticking. The dog is barking. The sprinklers are sprinkling. That crazy neighbor is chain-sawing at six in the morning!

Spiritually speaking, we have awoken to a world at war. You and I are caught in the middle of a cosmic collision, a battle for the ages, a historic clash that has been waged for centuries and generations. It is a confrontation between two kingdoms, and the battle is for the souls of people.

This war is real, and satan is not shooting rubber bullets. Since his mutiny in the Garden, lucifer has been feverishly working to snake-oil the Kingdom of Heaven. He resents who we represent, and we are caught in the middle of his personal vendetta against our King. We must remain sober and alert, lest we become a casualty of this war.

No kingdom is ever established without war, including the kingdom of darkness, yet no kingdom stands immune to enemy forces. In this section, we uncover two battle plans launched against the Kingdom of God and offer ways to aggressively triumph over them.

CHAPTER 11

INFILTRATION

"This is my kingdom. If I don't fight for it, who will?"
—Simba from *The Lion King*

I N the parable of the wheat and tares, Jesus tells of a farmer who plants wheat in his field, but while his servants sleep an enemy covertly sows false grain among the wheat. As the crop matures, the workers realize tares are growing in the field. They ask if they should uproot the tares, but the master replies, *"No, lest while you gather up the tares you also uproot the wheat with them."* Instead, he instructs them to permit both to grow until harvest time, at which time they should gather, bind, and burn up the tares but store the wheat in the barn (see Matt. 13:24-30).

We don't often get the luxury of a private interpretation of one of Jesus' parables, but here we do. In Matthew 13, the Teacher explains that the field represents the world, the farmer the Son of Man, the wheat the sons of the Kingdom, and the tares satan's subjects. At the end of the age, the Lord will order His harvesting angels to weed out of His Kingdom all that offends and those who practice lawlessness. He will cast them into the fire, but the righteous will shine like the sun in the Father's Kingdom (see Matt. 13: 36-43).

A wise king sifts out the wicked, and brings the threshing wheel over them (Proverbs 20:26).

There is much to learn about the Kingdom from this parable. First, it is apparent that the devil is at work in the Kingdom of God. He is shrewd, you know. He likes to piggyback a move of God so he can hurt it, pervert it, and divert it. It's the old, "If you can't beat 'em, join 'em" strategy. Jesus plainly identifies the tares as "sons of the wicked," indicating that hell's intention is to birth an offspring of false teachers, false prophets, and false doctrine among us (see Matt. 13:38). Christ is forewarning us. Evil will infiltrate our ranks.

It is not by chance that the character of this age seeks to mock the righteous and belittle the upright. Every day in the media we see evidence of a calculated assault on all that is pure and innocent. Places that should be safe like the womb, the home, the church, the campus, and the workplace are no longer so. This is a work of the devil and a result of lawlessness.

We cannot pretend that the father of lies bears no responsibility for the state of the planet. Long ago in the Garden, the devil somehow swindled the snake into letting him come in for a quick bite. He was the puppeteer working the strings of Haman with Mordecai, Jezebel with Elijah, Sanballat with Nehemiah, Judas with Jesus, Elymas with Paul, Nero with the church, and Hitler with the Jews. Your world is not immune either. There are people, words, and ideas literally on assignment from hell with the sole purpose of undermining the work of God in and around you.

Once I went through a difficult season of discouragement, and I was asking the Holy Spirit, "Why am I under such heavy spiritual attack?" To be honest, I was more complaining than praying, but He obliged and said, "Because the devil believes the prophecies spoken over you more than you do." How true it was and is. Our adversary is well aware of our potential in Christ, and he dreads the day we wake up and realize that together we are mightier than he.

Kingdom of Niceness

Jesus' story recounts that *while men slept,* the enemy crept in. Most would agree that the church is guilty of indulgence and indolence to some degree, but I believe this parable is addressing more than our work ethic or vigilance. After all, sleep is a necessary activity for workers. Jesus is alerting us to the stealth nature of darkness. Darkness has a way of creeping in subtly and undetected. Like a sleeper cell, it aims to amalgamate itself into the culture of the Kingdom for the purpose of terrorizing it.

Daniel speaks of the antichrist, saying *"...he shall corrupt with flattery,"* hinting that one of satan's most devious vices is a flattering tongue (Dan. 11:32). Don't you get the idea that the man of sin will come across as an extremely likeable guy? He will be magnetically sly, having a way with words and a way with people. Many will fall prey to his hypnotic ruse.

If this is true for the antichrist, then it is true for the spirit of the antichrist currently at work in the world. The enemy would like nothing better than to win our trust through flattery. Those among us who have need of being verbally stroked will be susceptible to this smooth-talking snake.

Why is it that most mass murderers are described by their neighbors as "quiet and nice"? It's because nice people can be vicious, violent, vindictive, and volatile behind their good manners. Paul foresaw ravenous wolves coming in to destroy the flock, and Jesus warned of false prophets cleverly disguised as trick-or-treating sheep knocking at the door of the church (see Acts 20:29; Matt. 7:15). When the motive is to manipulate, niceness can be as treacherous as treason.

Even cold-hearted killers prefer nice people, because nice people are safe. They neither make waves nor threaten darkness. Our adversary wants to reduce us to being a kingdom of zoo-kept animals, caged and tame; meanwhile he goes on wreaking havoc behind the scenes. But the Kingdom of God is more savage than suburban. Being nice is not a fruit of the Spirit, and the call to the Kingdom is a call to arms. We are not called to be nice; we are called to be kind and dangerous.

Growing a Star

When I was a boy, I had a fascination with star thistles. I thought it would be fun to have one as a plant, so one day I set out to grow my very own. After painstakingly extracted a thistle seed, I planted it in a pot and placed it in the sunniest part of our courtyard. I faithfully watered it each day and checked it for growth, but day after day nothing sprouted. Over time, I lost interest and figured I had a black thumb. Yikes, I couldn't even grow a weed!

A few weeks later, however, without water or attention, the thistle grew on its own. It began to sprout at the most surprising moment and at an alarming rate. The weed flourished once I had neglected the pot and deprived it of water.

The same is true with evil. We do not have to go looking for trouble. Trouble in the form of tares has a way of finding us. It is usually when we least expect it that darkness raises his ugly head in our midst. The minute we become distracted and careless and deny ourselves the sustenance of the Word, the enemy sprouts among us.

Tare Tactics

Notice that the tares appeared only at harvest time. It is not until the grain is about to yield an increase that the devil goes public with his intentions. He endeavors to intercept those entering the Kingdom of God, because he is after the crop. While the enemy hates you, he hopes to ruin more than just your life and your faith. He intends to use your demise to devastate your family, your marriage, your ministry, and your church, and simultaneously dilute the potency of God's Kingdom worldwide.

I know of a church overseas that was one of the most well-established churches of its nation. They had a functional building and committed members and provided leadership for other churches. I observed firsthand the Spirit of God begin a fresh work among them. People were getting saved, healed, delivered, filled with the Holy Spirit, ignited, and revived.

Suddenly, however, the pastor's wife started exerting control over the church. When her husband was absent, she would publicly rebuke people, tell the youth whom they could and couldn't marry, and teach things contrary to the Word of God. The men of the church united, rose up, and started praying for the church. They even once had to lock the gates of the church in order to keep her from stealing church property.

She convinced her husband to contact the secret police and accuse the men of rallying to form a rebellion to forcefully take over the church. When the secret police arrived unannounced on a Sunday morning, they had with them a list of names they had come to arrest. They read off each name, one by one, and commanded them to stand publicly and identify themselves. As each man's name was called, however, the whole congregation stood, so that the police could not determine which person it was. In that manner, they protected each other's identity. It was a beautiful picture of Christ's church laying it on the line and being willing to risk imprisonment for one another. The secret service agents were so astonished that no one was arrested that day. Unfortunately, it didn't stop the pastor couple from continuing to damage the church.

Satan seems completely satisfied with a lifeless, fruitless body of believers, but he gets nervous when believers come together and contend for the Kingdom of God. When we start loving each other, preaching the gospel, and threatening the population of hell, he calls his tare army to come to attention for the purpose of tearing us apart. Jealously arises, integrity fails, control issues surface, and people jockey for position. All too often during times of great harvest, we bicker over who gets the credit, who gets the converts, and who gets the cash. A study of church history reveals that we are most vulnerable to satan's vices when the harvest is ripe.

It is our testimony and unity that most threatens the enemy. The ruling spirit of Philippi was intimidated when Paul and Silas came to town, but it was only after Lydia and her household were baptized that the psychic girl set out to mock them. She pretended to promote the apostles to latch onto their anointing and undermine their credibility, but Paul saw through her smokescreen (see Acts 16). In similar fashion, the enemy will fasten himself onto a pure move of God to distort its message and discredit its testimony. His goal is to introduce a different gospel and an alternative Jesus when we are not looking. We must take caution with whom we yoke ourselves, because hell's con artist is snooping around looking for an open door to the Kingdom through alliances.

If you want to smoke out the enemy in your midst, boldly preach the Word of God with conviction and power. It is like "devil kryptonite." And be encouraged. If you uncover some tares in the process, know that you are on the cusp of a move of God. You must be doing something right. Keep at it.

Sadly, the story of that church is not too different from many others who had to endure something similar. Each time it happens, we all suffer from it but good still prevails for those who love the Lord. The silver lining of that situation was that it lit a fire in the people of God. They were even more committed to each other and determined to stand for truth, even if it cost them their lives. Sometimes it takes conflict to make a clear distinction between the wheat and the tares.

Tare Value

Jesus states that the master would not allow his servants to destroy the tares until the appointed time (Matt. 13:28-29). This is a puzzling strategy. Why not uproot the tares immediately? Why allow this evil to remain? The answer is baffling but brilliant—tares actually help advance the cause they mean to hinder.

Because Christ is Lord of all, even tares are subject to the reign of Christ, even though they are a work of the devil. One reason why God allows evil to remain is that you and I *need* tares in our life. The friction they create actually helps tighten our grip on the Kingdom.

When professional athletes want to strengthen their bodies, they don't go on vacation. They go into training. They understand that strength comes through exertion and resistance. The same is true in the Kingdom. Spiritual warfare is your training ground for greatness. You need a measure of resistance in your life, because the exertion it takes to engage the enemy serves to strengthen your spiritual muscles. Spurgeon put it this way, "Let satan do what he may, he only speeds on the cause which he desires to hinder."[1]

Tares have value. They test us and tend to divide us, but they eventually reveal those who are children of the Kingdom and those who are not. *"For there must also be factions among you, that those who are approved may be recognized among you"* (1 Cor. 11:19). Even the attack of the enemy serves a redemptive purpose in God's Kingdom.

Paul agrees with this notion, writing, "*...all who desire to live godly in Christ Jesus will suffer persecution*" (2 Tim. 3:12). This is not the kind of promise we post on our refrigerators as our power verse for the day. We usually don't pray, "Yes, Lord. I want to be persecuted today!" But truthfully, it is impossible to live a victorious Kingdom life without being persecuted. When we invoke God, we automatically provoke the devil, and it is this provocation that accelerates our journey toward Christlikeness.

When I first began to travel as an itinerant minister, I had to quickly learn that not everyone was going to like me or what I had to say, including fellow believers. One time at a Christian school I got kicked out of the pulpit by an angry dean of students. The man approached me in the middle of my sermon, and whispered in my ear, "I'll take it from here." Not wanting to create a scene and get in a tug-of-war match over the microphone, I surrendered the mic and sat down. He then led the rest of the meeting.

After the service, he and the worship leader thoroughly rebuked me for teaching the youth about the person of the Holy Spirit. Instead of arguing, I apologized for offending them and left. On the car ride home, I was distraught. I prayed, "Father, I am so sorry. Was I out of line? Are you disappointed with me?" I began to repent and ask for forgiveness.

The Lord responded by saying, "Why are you repenting? I didn't rebuke you. Keep preaching the Word." These words emboldened me. I was determined not to allow that experience to discourage me or sway me from proclaiming God's truth. That day served to solidify my faith and my call, and what the enemy meant for harm actually served to strengthen my resolve.

Your Persecution Is Your Promotion

What is often labeled spiritual warfare is merely spiritual development. The goal of spiritual warfare is not to get out of it but to get stronger through it. The Psalmist writes, "*[He] trains my hands for war, and my fingers for battle*" (Ps. 144:1). Saul served as David's crucible. He helped make David a warrior, and there is no warrior without a war; without a battle there is no champion.

I once read that wheat fields and vineyards differ greatly. Whereas grapes need water to grow, grain needs sunlight and lots of it. A wheat farmer will often measure the percentage of moisture remaining and use it as a yardstick to determine when the harvest is ripe. The stalk and root must be thoroughly dry before reaping. Direct sunlight, even in its severity, helps to mature and ripen wheat.[2]

From time to time, you and I must face the scorching severity of tribulation, but these trials are designed to ripen our faith and position our souls to photosynthesize of Word of God. The Lord permits them not only for our good but also for the good of His Kingdom. Persecution has an uncanny way of divorcing us from friendship with the world and drying us out to the worship of pleasure. Just as crops do not grow without sunlight, so our spiritual muscles tend to atrophy without resistance.

The same sunlight that ripens fruit, however, can also be devastating to a plant without roots. If young believers are not rooted and grounded in love, the persecution that dries them out to the desires of the world can also dry them up in their pursuit of the Kingdom. D.M. Panton writes, "Wheat dries towards earth but ripens toward Heaven."[3] The wheat of the world will find their strength to endure only by setting their gaze on Christ. When you disciple new converts, direct them to look up, for only in the light of God's face will the fruit of the Spirit be brought to complete maturity.

Here Comes the Pride

Tares are like cheap underwear—they just creep up on you. They can be next to impossible to detect, both in others and in our hearts. The Greek word for tare is *zizanion*. In Hebrew the word is *zonin*. One Jewish scholar writes that *zonin* is "a poisonous rye-grass which looks like wheat until the heads appear." It is "not a different plant from wheat but a degenerate form of it."[4] *Zizania* is particularly dangerous because if it gets mixed in and baked with the wheat, the bread becomes poisonous.[5] Wheat farmers tell us that the wheat and the tare are totally indistinguishable even at two feet tall. Even seasoned farmers cannot discern them. It is not until the fruit appears that they reveal their true colors. During harvest, the tare stands tall and black while the wheat bows and turns golden.

Jesus makes it clear that on Judgment Day the wicked will be purged from among the righteous, just as a shepherd separates goats from sheep. The degenerate will have a black heart that stands tall and haughty, but those with a golden heart will bow low in worship. I pray that you and I will be the ones found with a humble heart on that day. As well, I pray that the fruit of our ministries will be both vast and long-lasting.

Scandalous Affairs

Jesus concludes this parable by stating that He will "...*send out His angels, and they will gather out of His kingdom all things that offend, and those who practice lawlessness*" (Matt. 13:41). *Offend* in Greek is *skandalon*, from which we derive the word *scandal*. The indication here is that our adversary seeks to riddle the Kingdom of God with offenses and scandalous behavior.

> *Woe to the world because of offenses (**skandalon**)! For offenses must come, but woe to that man by whom the offense comes* (Matthew 18:7).

*Now I urge you, brethren, note those who cause divisions and offenses (**skandalon**), contrary to the doctrine which you learned, and avoid them (Romans 16:17).*

*They have no root in themselves, and so endure only for a time. Afterward, when tribulation or persecution arises for the word's sake, immediately they stumble (**skandalizo**) (Mark 4:17).*

*And if your eye causes you to sin (**skandalizo**), pluck it out. It is better for you to enter the kingdom of God with one eye, rather than having two eyes, to be cast into hell fire (Mark 9:47).*

*...Balaam...taught Balak to put a stumbling block (**skandalon**) before the children of Israel...(Revelation 2:14).*

Webster defines a scandal as "the unseemly conduct of a religious person that discredits religion or causes moral lapse in another," and "any act, person, or thing that offends or shocks moral feelings of the community and leads to disgrace."[6]

Without question, scandals have tainted the image of Christ to those we mean to reach. People are furious at corruption in politics, sports, media, government, and the church, and rightly so. There is no way around it. We are absolutely responsible for scandals among us. One day we will have to give an account before the throne of God, so let judgment begin with the house of God. We must judge ourselves first before we can ever judge angels.

Infiltration System

The life of Daniel provides a model on how to resist satan's infiltration. Daniel knew well about enemy occupation. As a teenager, he was taken as a prisoner of war and forced to serve in the palace of King Nebuchadnezzar when Jerusalem was invaded by the Babylonians in 605 B.C.[7] Babylon sought to reprogram him, educating him in pagan customs and teaching him the language of the Chaldeans. He was given the name Belteshazzar, the name of a Babylonian god. But Daniel (whose name means "God is my Judge") purposed in his heart not to defile himself with the wine and delicacies from the king's table, and the Lord honored him for it.

The Lord gave him unprecedented understanding, wisdom, and skill, beyond anyone else in the king's courts. He possessed superior prophetic abilities, even revealing and interpreting the dreams of emperors. His favor and authority spanned three kingdoms, and he was given some of the most profound insights of the Kingdom of God. Today, we remember Daniel as Daniel, not Belteshazzer, because he refused to allow Babylon to infiltrate the kingdom of his heart.

Babylon means "confusion by mixture," and this same Babylon is at work today. It seeks to bring mixture to the Kingdom of God by captivating our attention, confusing us about our identity, and educating us in the ways of the world. Time spent at the altar of materialism, gazing at pornography, or paying homage to pagan holy days is time spent in Babylon's classroom. It is through this education that the enemy seeks to reprogram us.

But there is a generation of Daniels who refuse to be defined by Wall Street, Hollywood, or the Vatican. They are defenders of the faith, defeaters of the flesh, and reflectors of the glory. God is their Judge, and Babylon is their enemy. They have found that the intoxications of the world are distasteful in light of the blessings of God.

For 15 years, I have not owned a television. When Meljoné and I got married, we decided to not have a television in our home for the first year of our marriage. Not once did we feel like we were missing out. In fact, it was so successful that we continued to live without a television year after year. People thought we were a bit extreme. It would get worse.

The Holy Spirit then led us to stop celebrating Christmas and Easter and to be intentional about observing Sabbath. We now celebrate the feasts of the Lord as Jesus and the early church did. Needless to say, it created quite a stir in our families, especially around holiday time. We were not trying to make a statement or make things difficult for them but simply trying to be obedient to the leading of the Lord.

Since we have made those decisions, we have sensed the presence of God in our home in tangible ways. Once while we were praying in the Sabbath, a wind blew through our kitchen. It was strong enough to cause Meljoné's hair to blow, and both of us could feel a cool breeze on our face. I checked to see if there were any open windows in the house, and sure enough there was one—a window from Heaven. For us, these decisions were not compulsory acts but voluntary expressions of our devotion to Christ.

Daniel's life bears witness that those without mixture will be given a greater measure of wisdom, understanding, authority, and revelation in the Kingdom of God. If his life were told as a parable, Daniel would be the wheat and Babylon the tares. In this parable, however, God turns the tables on the accuser. Daniel is the wheat planted in satan's turf. He was a tare terrorist, invading the enemy's territory and captivating the attention of a generation.

In the same way, you are God's special agent infiltrating the world with truth, righteousness, and the Kingdom of God. The way to overcome satan's infiltration system is to infiltrate it with a greater Kingdom. When the wicked brush up next to us, we should not be afraid of defilement. Instead, they should be the one walking away with a taste of our Heaven.

Conclusion

The Kingdom of God stands as the last remaining force against rebellion and oppression on earth. According to this parable, we can be assured that evil will be present in the world until the end of the age. All our efforts of world peace will prove only short-lived, for there will never be world peace until the Prince of Peace rules the world.

At the end of this parable, Jesus reveals a profound truth not seen at first glance. He says,

The Son of Man will send out His angels, and they will gather ***out of His kingdom*** *all things that offend, and those who prac-tice lawlessness, and will cast them into the furnace of fire. There will be wailing and gnashing of teeth. Then the righteous will shine forth as the sun* ***in the kingdom of their Father.*** *He who has ears to hear, let him hear* (Matthew 13:41-43).

Whereas in the beginning of the parable the field represents the world, in the end it represents the Kingdom of God. And this is the truth worth pondering: *the world is succumbing to the Kingdom of God.* Christ is claiming the nations of the world as His own. *"The kingdoms of the world have become the Kingdom of our Lord and of His Christ, and He shall reign forever and ever"* (Rev. 11:15). Even satan's domain will become God's great domain.

There is coming a great day when the kingdom of darkness will col-lapse and be cast out of the Kingdom of Heaven. It will be announced with a shout, for it will be a glorious day. On that day, the culmination of God's Kingdom and our salvation will be complete.

Then I heard a loud voice saying in Heaven, "Now salvation, and strength, and the Kingdom of our God, and the power of His Christ have come, for the accuser of our brethren, who accused them before our God day and night, has been cast down" (Revelation 12:10).

Endnotes

1. Ray Comfort, *How To Win Souls & Influence People* (Bridge-Logos Publishing: New Brunswick, NJ, 1999), 122

2. Watchman Nee, *The King And The Kingdom* (New York, NY: Christian Fellowship Publishers, Inc., 1978), 152.

3. Ibid.

4. David H. Stern, *Jewish New Testament Commentary* (Clarksville, MD: Jewish New Testament Publications, Inc., 1992), 48.

5. Chuck Missler, *The Book of Revelation Audio Series Session*, CD 8.

6. *Webster's New World Dictionary,* s.v. "Scandal."

7. Herbert Lockyer, *Nelson's Illustrated Bible Dictionary* (Nashville, TN: Thomas Nelson Publishers, 1986), PC Study Bible Version.

CHAPTER 12

GNOSTICISM

"To you it has been granted to know the mysteries of the Kingdom of Heaven."
(Matthew 13:11 NASB)

GOD is a mystery. The Author of Life is an uncreated, unpredictable, and undomesticated Genius. He is neither a formula to be calculated nor a principle to be ascertained; He is transcendent, transrational, and at times absolutely ambiguous.

Our small minds can never conquer the Almighty, for He does not bow to our feeble deductions and reductions. He cannot be tamed like an animal or mastered like an art. Whenever we try to put God in a box, a resurrection always take place, and that vacated space returns to being just an empty tomb.

> *"For My thoughts are not your thoughts, nor are your ways My ways," says the Lord. "For as the heavens are higher than the earth, so are My ways higher than your ways, and My thoughts than your thoughts"* (Isaiah 55:8-9).

There is nothing more thrilling than to entertain the thought of an eternal Being, and what comes to our minds when we think about God reveals the most about us.[1] How we view God directly affects how we view ourselves, yet with every "God encounter" we are left with mountains of new questions. A mature believer must be comfortable living with this paradox.

Mystery Machine

The human soul is prewired to be intrigued by mystery. Whether a "whodunit" detective novel, a psychological thriller, or an episode of *Scooby Doo,* we find great satisfaction in following clues that lead us to the truth. What relief we gain when we learn that it was Professor Plum in the conservatory with the candlestick!

What is it about a mystery that fascinates us? Is it the chase, the prize, or both? A mystery is much like Shakespeare. Although we never fully grasp it, it never lets us go.

Our Inventor has purposely sown eternal curiosity into the fabric of the human heart. He is still in the business of employing bright stars, burning bushes, and manna burgers to cause the bewildered to ask, "What is it?"[2] Through ambiguity the spiritual voyager is left captivated, and through mystery he is drawn into deeper waters.

Insider Information

Like God, the Kingdom of Heaven is mysterious. Jesus likened it to the miracle of a sprouting seed or the adventure of a treasure hunt. The disciples asked Jesus why He spoke to the crowds in parables, and He replied:

> ...*Because it has been given to you to know the mysteries of the kingdom of Heaven, but to them it has not been given. For whoever has, to him more will be given, and he will have abundance; but whoever does not have, even what he has will be taken away from him. Therefore I speak to them in parables...*(Matthew 13:11-13).

The Master states that not all who hear the Kingdom message will grasp it. Prophetic insight and Kingdom comprehension seem to be the reward of those who hang out with the King. According to Jesus, understanding is a gift from Heaven, and the more we have it the more we will be given.

As seekers of the Kingdom, we have been afforded the opportunity of a lifetime—to know what is unknown to the common person. We have been given access to privileged information. We are insiders now, no longer on the outside of God's plan looking in. He has chosen to share with us the mysteries of what He is preparing the world for in Christ.

A False Mystery

This is where the devil enters from stage left. Since he is not a creator, he is reduced to the work of fabrication, forgery, and perversion, and he has forged a counterfeit mystery called Gnosticism.

Gnosticism is an ancient doctrine rooted in the Tree of Knowledge. In Genesis 3, lucifer convinced Eve that God was obstructing humankind from a secret wisdom found only in the forbidden fruit. This divine wisdom was promised through the gateway of knowledge and could only be realized by pursuing knowledge above obedience to God's commands. This is the deception of Gnosticism.

The word *Gnosticism* comes from the Greek word *gnosis,* which means "mystical knowledge or enlightenment."[3] Gnostics claim to possess a secret knowledge about the spirit world that has been kept hidden from the general public. They believe that salvation comes through private information, which is concealed and contrary to revealed truth. This spiritual intelligence is unfit for the vulgar crowd, but set apart for a superior class of beings—the elect, the enlightened, the informed.

Gnostic cosmology maintains that the world is imperfect because it was created in a faulty manner. It concludes that the creator, not creation, bears the responsibility and blame for our suffering and pain.[4] One school of Gnosticism designates Demiurgos as the creator of the earth. Demiurgos is characterized as a malevolent tyrant, said to be the offspring of Sophia (wisdom), a female deity. She birthed this half-god by mistake, which explains why the world is flawed.[5]

Early Gnostic writings teach that Jehovah is just another name for Demiurgos. They describe him as rigid, lacking compassion, prone to genocide, and selfish for kicking knowledge-seeking humankind out of the Garden.[6] The serpent, still honored in Gnostic writings today, is the hero of the Genesis account, because he liberated humankind from the oppression of this evil god.[7]

Classic Gnosticism is arguably nothing more than thinly disguised pantheism. It teaches a radical dualism between spirit and matter. It maintains that the material world is a deterioration of the spiritual world and that all matter is evil. Because man is both physical and spiritual, Gnostics conclude that the spirit of a man is good but his body is wicked. Among other things, Gnostics feel imprisoned by their own bodies.[8]

This dualism placed the traditional Gnostic disciple on one of two journeys. The conservative was ultra ascetic, punishing and tormenting the body with cruel legalism. Some were vegans; others became celibate. The liberal Gnostics, however, were ultra-perverse, indulging themselves in every known pleasure. To them, morality was relative and not relevant to salvation. It mattered not what they did in the body, because they believed their spirit was inherently good. Incredibly, some Gnostics found themselves practicing both asceticism and debauchery![9]

Today, Gnostics are a loosely organized group holding a diversity of beliefs. Modern Gnostic doctrine is vast and relative to one's spiritual experiences, but its underlying theme is uniform: *to exalt itself above the knowledge of God.* Most Gnostics believe that divinity is within, and in order to become spiritual they must shed the physical. To the true Gnostic, death liberates the soul and releases the divine spark, so long as there is substantial work of gnosis undertaken before death. If not, the divine spark is hurled back to earth and enslaved once again to a physical body.[10]

Christian Gnosticism

Christian Gnosticism blends intellectual paganism with the teachings of the apostles. It boasts of being the only true form of Christianity and claims to possess a pure and clandestine interpretation of the teachings of Jesus.

Christian Gnostics reject the idea that salvation comes by grace through faith in Christ. They assert that eternal life can only be attained when the spirit becomes awakened by knowledge. What is more, Gnostics generally have no concept of sin, except the sin of ignorance. Therefore, Christ's sufferings bring no benefit to humanity. As long as Gnostics are spiritual, they will be saved irrespective of their behavior.[11]

Many first-century Gnostics adhered to the doctrine of Docetism, which rejects the humanity of Christ. Because Gnostics hold that the body is wicked, they concluded that Christ could never inhabit flesh and blood and was merely a phantom that only appeared human. This meant that Jesus' death on the Cross was apparent, but not actual. Some even insisted that Simon of Cyrene took the place of Jesus on the cross.[12]

Obviously, the Gnostic savior is entirely different from the Biblical Savior. Let's contrast the two.

Biblical Savior	Gnostic Savior
Fully God, fully man	Was superhuman without a human nature
Saves people from sin	Saves people from ignorance
Atoned for our sin through His blood	Atoned nothing
Was sent for the benefit of humanity	Brings no benefit to humanity except good teaching
Sufferings were for our healing	Sufferings were in vain
Uncreated	Birthed by Sophia (Isis)
Was born of a virgin	Was merely an apparition
Was tortured, crucified, and buried	Created an illusion that he was being crucified
Resurrected from the grave	Just appeared and disappeared

Without a doubt, Gnosticism attempts to call into question the Lordship of Jesus Christ. Our adversary wants to discredit the integrity of Jesus so as to discredit the power of His message. Once the truth of Christ is compromised, all truth becomes relative. It is only a matter of time before people cast off restraint and plunge into depravity.

The early apostles, including Paul and John, rejected Gnostic writings because they contained doctrines contrary to the credibility of Scripture and the teachings of Christ. After the resurrection, the early church had to contend with this heresy.

Power Over the People

There is some debate about where New Testament Gnosticism found its origins. Some have noted Nicolas as perhaps one of its early proponents. Nicolas was a proselyte from Antioch and a contemporary of the Twelve. Along with several others, he was chosen to help oversee the food distribution of the Hellenist widows in the early Jerusalem church. He was described as a good man, full of the Holy Spirit and wisdom, which were the criteria for the job, but some believe he took a wrong turn doctrinally and morally (see Acts 6:1-6).

Scripture is silent on the matter, but it does mention a heretical sect called the Nicolaitans that arose within the early church. They either followed or perverted the teachings of one named Nicolas. In Revelation 2, Jesus commends the church of Ephesus for rejecting the deeds of the Nicolaitans, which He says He hates. He then rebukes the next church for holding to the doctrine of the Nicolaitans and not detesting their deeds. It is here that Jesus links the works of the Nicolaitans with the doctrine of Balaam.

The name *Nicolas* means "conqueror of the people," and *Nicolaitan* means "power over the laity."[13] Whoever this original Nicolas was it seems he had the ability to exert power over people. We cannot speculate whether Nicolas of Acts is responsible for introducing Gnosticism to the church or not, but we can know with certainty that the enemy still tries to implant these ideals within our fellowships. Through idolatry, sexual immorality, divination, and false doctrine, Gnosticism threatens to compromise the moral fabric of the Kingdom.

John the apostle identifies the spirit behind Gnosticism as the spirit of the antichrist, saying:

> *Beloved, do not believe every spirit, but test the spirits, whether they are of God; because many false prophets have gone out into the world. By this you know the Spirit of God: Every spirit that confesses that Jesus Christ has come in the flesh is of God, and every spirit that does not confess that Jesus Christ has come in the flesh is not of God. And this is the spirit of the Antichrist, which you have heard was coming, and is now already in the world (1 John 4:1-3).*

Conspiracy Theory

Today, we are seeing the ugly head of Gnosticism rise again. Visit any modern bookstore and you will find countless books promoting Gnostic ideas and alternative views on the life of Jesus: *The Acts of Thomas,* "The Secret Book of James," *The Lost Gospel of Mary,* and the newly uncovered *Gospel of Judas.* What's next, the Gospel of the Thief on the Cross? It seems with Gnostics you only need to be a biblical figure to have your own gospel!

Gnostic writings have found a revival within the secular community as a substitute to the firsthand accounts of the resurrection of Christ. The devil has effectively concocted a conspiracy theory, suggesting that somehow the real truth about Jesus of Nazareth is hidden in some code; that He really was married with children and that His bones can be found in a remote grave outside of Jerusalem. These conclusions always cast doubt on the identity of Jesus and attempt to repudiate the empty tomb.[14]

This should not threaten us though. Our faith is strong enough to be challenged, for it is not based on flakey archaeology or fabricated history. The Bible possesses overwhelming archaeological, scientific, and eyewitness merit.

Recently, I struck up a conversation with a flight attendant on a flight coming from Dallas. The Holy Spirit began to impress on my heart certain things to share with her as I spoke to her about Christ. As the Lord was pinpointing her heart, suddenly a man appeared and interrupted our conversation. He overhead us talking and began to challenge my words and my doctrine. He quoted the Gospel of Thomas, saying that Jesus told Thomas in private that salvation really comes by knowing the god inside of all of us. When this man began to speak of the Gnostic gospels the flight attendant perked up, saying, "That sounds so fascinating. I want to read the Gnostic gospels and learn more about the secret things." After a spirited conversation, he returned to his seat, and she had no more interest in what I had to say.

Satan is shrewd. Just as he manipulated Eve's God-given desire for wisdom, he used this flight attendant's God-given desire for mystery to lead her astray. Gnostic thought is responsible for leading many down unlighted paths. It is believed to have influenced secret societies such as Freemasonry, the Knights Templar, and the Illuminati.[13]

It is not that knowledge and mystery have no place in the Kingdom. In fact, the opposite is true. Mystery is vital, and knowledge is to be cherished. It is when we allow them to govern our salvation that they betray us. Both mystery and knowledge should make truth more absolute, Scripture more relevant, and the resurrection a historical fact. They should lead people closer to the deity of Christ, not further away.

Any experienced money handler will tell you that the way to recognize a counterfeit is by having a feel for the real. The presence of a counterfeit is merely evidence that the genuine exists and has value. Gnosticism is a counterfeit mystery, and we need not fear it so long as we remain a student of the authentic Kingdom of God. Gnostic deception should not spook us away from the mysteries and knowledge of God but rather cause us to gravitate toward them. The way we combat a false mystery is by becoming stewards of the genuine mysteries of God (see 1 Cor. 4:1).

Gnosticism thrives on scandals and secretive behavior, but the truth is there is no secret to uncover. There is no code to crack, no conspiracy to contend with, and no controversial archeological evidence to unearth. When Jesus gave up His Spirit on the Cross, eyewitnesses record that the veil of the temple which separated the holy of holies from the inner court was torn in two (see Matt. 27:51). This happened to demonstrate that the presence of God is no longer exclusive. We all have equal access to God through our Great High Priest Jesus Christ.

> *Now to Him who is able to establish you according to my gos-pel and the preaching of Jesus Christ, according to the revela-tion of the mystery kept secret since the world began but now made manifest, and by prophetic Scriptures made known to all nations, according to the commandment of the everlasting God, for obedience to the faith* (Romans 16:25-26).

Trade Secrets

Faith is what distinguishes New Testament salvation from Gnosticism. One has faith in Christ; the other has faith in knowledge. One operates in mystery; the other in secrets. The difference between a secret and a mystery is that a secret is told with the intention that it be kept hidden, but a mystery is meant to be discovered. God's Kingdom is not a secret society. It is a mystery, an ancient treasure map that leads to an endless supply of spiritual riches. It does not require a secret name, password, or handshake to enter it but only a heart of faith set on obedience.

Why then did Jesus admit to passing insider information? Why did He mask His message from the masses? Why conceal truth instead of reveal it? Why not just proclaim, "Here I am! God's Son, the King. Worship Me?"

My daughter loves to play hide and seek. As a toddler, she would hunt for Mommy and Daddy around the house, and when she found us she would giggle and say, "Ahhh." Truthfully, I play the game with her not just because she loves it, but because I love it too. To the see the wonder on her face when she finds me is priceless, and the bond that a simple chase brings to our relationship is profound.

In the same way, perhaps the Father has hidden truth from us so that we would search Him out in the process. Life is not a game to Him, yet He wants to be wanted. Our passionate pursuit of our Father and His passionate pursuit of us is the thrill of the Kingdom. As we seek first the Kingdom of God, we are creating an everlasting bond with our Heavenly Daddy. To those who have no love for truth, truth remains concealed, but eyes and ears are given to those who are sincere seekers of truth. In this way, God protects eternal truth from abuse.

Jesus intentionally hid His Kingdom, but not because He intended it to remain hidden; rather, He wants it explored. The secret is out. Jesus is alive, and He is the answer. He said, *"there is nothing covered that will not be revealed, and hidden that will not be known. Whatever I tell you in the dark, speak in the light; and what you hear in the ear, preach on the housetops"* (Matt. 10:26-27).

Mystery, Not Mastery

Most of our modern evangelism concentrates on how to defend the tenets of our faith and respond to certain questions. While this is beneficial and necessary, there is a more effective strategy than just answering a question (see 1 Pet. 3:15). It is answering the unspoken question.

Have you noticed that oftentimes Jesus didn't initially resolve the crisis that was presented to Him? A Gentile woman asks Jesus to heal her severely demon-possessed daughter (see Matt. 15:21-28). Blind Bartimaeus begs for mercy as the Healer walks by (see Mark 10:46-52). The disciples fearfully cry out thinking Jesus is a water-walking ghost (see Mark 6:47-50). In each of these instances, it appears that Jesus intended to pass them all by.

Was Jesus indifferent to their crisis? Did He turn a deaf ear to their suffering? No. In each of these stories all were delivered and comforted, but not due to their silence. It was their continual cry that arrested His attention.

Jesus is able to address a deeper need than just the felt need. He responds to the cry of the heart. The world is crying out for help, and what we need to present to the world is not so much a secret or an enlightened answer but a mystery. Our mission is not to be become experts on God through developing perfect doctrine and ironclad theologies. We are called to present the world with the mystery of Christ (see Col. 4:3). Our goal should never be the *mastery* of God but always the *mystery* of God, for only when people truly embrace God's mystery will they truly embrace His *majesty*.

A relationship with Christ devoid of mystery is always prone to the vices of religion. Even in light of Gnosticism, do not exclude this element of mystery from your message, for in it is veiled the hidden wisdom of God (see 1 Cor. 2:7).

> *Pray for us, too, that God may open a door for our message, so that we may proclaim the mystery of Christ...* (Colossians 4:3 NIV).

The mystery that Paul speaks of is the inclusion of Gentiles with Israel as fellow heirs of the promises of God. He called it the mystery of the gospel. He writes that the fellowship of this mystery has been hidden in God from the beginning of the ages but is now revealed so that we can understand the manifold wisdom of God (see Eph. 1:9; 3:9). God's universal Kingdom will culminate with Jew and Gentile together, and we Gentile outsiders are now insiders with God.

Conclusion

The human spirit is created with a deep yearning to be fascinated, and until the world discovers the truth of Christ as we have, they will never find rest. God's intent is that people become so intrigued and captivated by His creation that it leads them to encountering the Creator and His Kingdom.

God has now made known to us the mystery of His Kingdom come on earth. As Kingdom custodians, we are keepers of the heavenly treasures of wisdom, and hell has overplayed its hand once again. The knowledge of salvation is not top secret after all. The mystery has now been made manifest. The veil is removed. Truth has come out of the closet, and all have been invited to encounter God through Christ.

Endnotes

1. A.W. Tozer, *The Knowledge of the Holy* (New York, NY: Harper and Brothers, 1961), 9.

2. *Manna* in Hebrew means, "What is it?"

3. The Random House Dictionary, *Dictionary.com,* s.v. "Gnosis," definition 1, http://dictionary.reference.com/browse/gnosis (accessed April 03, 2009).

4. Stephan A. Hoeller, "The Gnostic World View: A Brief Summary of Gnosticism," The Gnosis Archive, http://www.gnosis.org/gnintro.htm (accessed April 03, 2009).

5. J.P. Arendzen, *The Catholic Encyclopedia*, VI. (New York, NY: Robert Appleton Company, 1909); s.v. "Gnosticism," http://www.newadvent.org/cathen/06592a.htm (accessed April 03, 2009); Stephan A. Hoeller, "The Gnostic World View: A Brief Summary of Gnosticism," The Gnosis Archive, http://www.gnosis.org/gnintro.htm (accessed April 03, 2009).

6. J.P. Arendzen, *The Catholic Encyclopedia*, VI. (New York, NY: Robert Appleton Company, 1909), s.v. "Gnosticism," http://www.newadvent.org/cathen/06592a.htm (accessed April 03, 2009); Edward Moore, *The Internet Encyclopedia of Philosophy,* s.v. "Gnosticism," http://www.utm.edu/research/iep/g/gnostic.htm (accessed April 3, 2009).

7. B.A. Robinson, "Gnosticism—Ancient and Modern," News and Issues from Bristol Virginia and Bristol Tennessee, http://www.sullivan-county.com/id2/gnostic_files/gnostic2.htm (accessed April 03, 2009).

8. J.P. Arendzen, *The Catholic Encyclopedia*, VI. (New York, NY: Robert Appleton Company, 1909), s.v. "Gnosticism," http://www.newadvent.org/cathen/06592a.htm (accessed April 03, 2009).

9. *Nelson's Illustrated Bible Dictionary* (Nashville: Thomas Nelson, 1986),

10. For more on Gnosticism, visit http://www.earlychristianwritings .com/gnostics.html, http://www.religioustolerance.org/gnostic .htm, and http://www.newadvent.org/cathen/06592a.htm.

11. Stephan A. Hoeller, "The Gnostic World View: A Brief Summary of Gnosticism," The Gnosis Archive, http://www.gnosis.org/gnintro. htm (accessed April 03, 2009).

12. Nicholas Carr, *Encyclopaedia Brittanica*, s.v. "Docetism," http:// www.britannica.com/EBchecked/topic/167323/Docetism (accessed April 3, 2009).

13. James Strong, *BibleSoft's New Exhaustive Strong's Numbers and Concordance with Expanded Greek-Hebrew Dictionary* (Nashville, TN: Thomas Nelson Inc., 1994),

15. (see Dan Brown, *The Da Vinci Code,* http://news.bbc. co.uk/2/hi/middle_east/6397373.stm, accessed April 30, 2009; http://dsc.discovery.com/news/2007/02/25/tomb_arc. html?category=archaeology, accessed April 30, 2009).

REIGNING IN THE KINGDOM

*"They shall be priests of God and of Christ,
and shall reign with Him a thousand years."*
(Revelation 20:6)

THE saints ruling with Christ is one of the most undertaught topics of the Bible, yet the narrative of the Kingdom is incomplete without this element. We all have a place at the table of this great domain. Now is our training ground for then, and as we are faithful, so we will be rewarded. Once God fully reigns *in* us, He can effectively reign *through* us.

In this last section, we discuss how Christ governs His Kingdom and what our role is in reigning with Him. He has given each a crown of authority, but it does not come without a responsibility. This responsibility is our opportunity for glory.

CHAPTER 13

BLUE-COLLAR PARADISE

"Unfortunately, the kingdom involvement of many Christians is of the video game variety. We play it, it requires a certain amount of attention, but we don't see it as a life-and-death situation, which may be why many believers walk away from their kingdom assignments expecting only to have sacrificed some small change."
—David Mains

T HERE a stunning view on the north coast of Maui that is surely one of the most breathtaking sights on earth. Meljoné and I stumbled across it while driving the famous road to Hana.

Facing the ocean, you can see miles and miles of white-sand beaches freckled with date palm trees all along the coast of this tropical island. I found myself perched on a tall rock watching silver waves shimmer under a saffron sunset near an old Spanish mission. Here, the warm ocean breeze kisses your face as it dances across a coconut grove and the sound of a distant honeycreeper can be heard singing to the rhythmic roar of the tides.

The view facing the island is just as spectacular. It exhibits a vast, tropical rainforest folded with crinkled valleys of lush, green ferns flanked by cedar groves, cypress trees, and endless gardens of exotic flowers. In the distance stands a majestic volcano mounted by strong mountains displaying spectacular waterfalls cascading down thousand-foot cliffs. Wow! No wonder Hawaii is called paradise. The "No Trespassing" sign was the only barrier keeping me from running uninhibited through this jungle sanctuary.

In both directions, the view offered untouched beauties and unconquered possibilities, but surprisingly it was not the scenery that kept me fascinated. It was the mystique of uncharted territory. As I peered out over the ocean to my left, I envisioned myself as Magellan navigating the seven seas. Gazing at the valley to my right, I wanted to fight off wild boars and ginormous spiders to reach the crest of the waterfall.

Even in the midst of such beauty, my heart yearned for something more than rest; it longed for the perils of the unexpected. What it craved was not a vacation, but an adventure.

Your Creator has fashioned you for spiritual expedition. Our souls yearn for something dangerous, something unconquered, something unpredictable. For many, life has become so bogged down with to do lists and trivial pursuits that if we really got honest we would confess that we are thoroughly bored with life.

What if there was a haven like Hawaii for our souls, a land of beauty and sacred discovery, a pursuit so adventurous, so radical, so purposeful that it beckons us to run uninhibited through the jungles of life? The truth is, there is.

The Lost World

The thief on the cross was one of the first to enter the Kingdom of Heaven. When he met the Lord at Golgotha on the final day of his life, he undoubtedly was familiar with the ministry of the Nazarene. Perhaps he had a relative who followed Yeshua, or he was one of the thousands who personally witnessed the healing touch of the Master. Maybe he was an attentive listener hanging on the Lord's every word, or perhaps the unruly cynic who balked at His teachings. Scripture does not elaborate, but it does say that he knew Jesus was a sinless man, unlike himself.

This thief was being punished for his crimes, and dying on a cross next to Jesus, said, *"Lord, remember me when You come into Your kingdom."* The Messiah's response to him is shocking. He replies, *"Assuredly, I say to you, today you will be with Me in Paradise."* The promised land for this man was a paradise kingdom (see Luke 23:39-43).

Paradise is a term not often found in Scripture. It is used only twice outside this verse, and both times it refers to a place in Heaven. The word *paradeisos* was commonly employed by the Persians to describe a shady and well-watered park. In those days, a paradise was a natural preserve enclosed by walls and towers and used as hunting grounds. *Paradeisos* also depicted a grove of trees or a pleasurable garden.[1] For all intents and purposes, paradise was spiritual Hawaii.

Jesus here equates paradise with the Kingdom of Heaven. He says to the penitent criminal that the King is coming into His Kingdom, and on that very day they would be together in paradise. The most unlikely man in history stumbled upon the greatest discovery of all time—the entryway to the lost paradise world of God. We now know that Jesus is the Lord of this paradise, and like this dying man on the cross we enter it when we take up our cross and acknowledge Jesus as Lord.

Paradise Needs a Gardener

God's original design for the planet was nothing short of paradise. In the Garden, the will of God and the purity of Heaven reigned supreme. Adam and Eve lived there in the lap of luxury, untamed and unashamed, without fear or stress. They were innocent and wise, intimate and free. Eden served as the earthly headquarters of Heaven. It was literally Heaven on earth—the first manifestation of the Kingdom of God.

God gave Adam an assignment. He was Heaven's diplomat on earth, representing and "re-presenting" God to all creation. His mission was to influence his world with the rule of God. He was given dominion over the plants, animals, and environment, and he had permission to eat the harvest of the ground, name the animals, and manage the globe. This was our Genesis Great Commission.

Surprisingly, Eden had no hammock. What I mean is that, while it was glorious, paradise was not a resort or an eternal retirement home. The first family did not lounge all day next to the fountain of youth sipping Eden-ade and working on their tan. God placed Adam in the Garden and gave him a job. *"...There was no man to till the ground...then the Lord God took the man and put him in the Garden of Eden to tend and keep it"* (Gen. 2:5,15). Evidently, paradise needed a gardener.

God's notion of paradise is not like ours, just as the Promised Land was not quite what the Israelites had envisioned. They were promised the jewel of the Middle East, with *"...fountains and springs, that flow out of valleys and hills"* (Deut. 8:7). At that time, the land of Canaan was a rich, fertile greenbelt that stretched along the eastern coast of the Mediterranean. It was spacious and magnificent, a land flowing with milk and honey. There they found grapes the size of plums and iron as common as stone (see Deut. 8:9).[2] Yet the place was crawling with intimidating giants and fortified cities. Inheriting this land would require courage, struggle, and war.

The children of Israel had to contend for their God-given domain. When the Lord promised a land flowing with milk and honey, it involved time, effort, and sacrifice. They would have to milk a few cows, raid a few beehives, and topple a few kingdoms in order to come into their inheritance. Likewise, entering our promised land requires similar effort.

Louis Nizer writes, "A man who works with his hands is a laborer; a man who works with his hands and his brain is a craftsman; but a man who works with his hands and his brains and his heart is an artist."[3] Life is art, but it takes a certain degree of labor in life for our dreams to become a reality.

God's promised land to us is blue-collar. It is not for the slothful but for the courageous, for those willing to roll up their sleeves and sweat. It is not to lounge in but to labor in. Neither is it an escape from reality, but rather a glorious baptism into it. Thomas Edison said, "Opportunity is missed by most people because it is dressed in overalls and looks like work."[4]

It has been said that there are two kinds of people in the world: those who do the work and those who take the credit for the work, and those who do the work have an easier time than those who take the credit because they face less competition. You have a job to do and an enemy to engage, and the Kingdom of God is your training ground. This is your space to rule and to conquer—your place to invest all your energies, ambitions, and aspirations. God's Kingdom is your garden and you are the gardener, and it rewards those who are willing to contend for it.

When I was in campus ministry, our local leadership was committed to team ministry. Each of us on staff had an assignment such as outreach to athletes, the community college, discipleship, prayer, missions, and small groups. My principal assignment was Chico State University. It was my promised land, my garden to tend, my place to invest time and energy. I took upon myself the responsibility to evangelize, disciple, and pray for the campus even if no one else did. I considered myself one of the spiritual guardians over the students, and I took it personally when my garden was neglected or taken advantage of.

One semester some independent campus evangelists stormed the campus, pointing fingers and calling students whores and faggots. They were purposely offensive, and I took it upon myself to confront the issue. Their presence created outrage, and I recognized that the enemy was trying to destroy the credibility of the gospel on campus. I was determined to turn it into an opportunity to present Christ, so I personally talked with many angry students about the incident and about Jesus. In the process, relationships were built, trust was restored, misconceptions were undone, and some came to Christ. Still, the community of believers lost some favor with the university for a time.

In your garden, you may have to take on Pharaoh, leave your Egypt and face a wilderness in order to come into the promises of God. You may labor and never reap. You may struggle and want to quit. You may toil with tears without ever fully occupying what is promised. And just when you thought you had given everything, the Lord may ask for more.

But let's face it. What we get for our struggle is not half as valuable as what we become. People who never do anything beyond what they are compensated for never receive compensation for anything more that what they do. To the person passionate about the Kingdom, nothing is laborious unless they would rather be doing something else. Nelson Boswell put it this way: "The most miserable man in the world is the one who has no work to dedicate himself to."[5]

The Toughest Job You Will Ever Love

Like paradise, God's idea of work is different from ours. Before the Fall, work was enjoyable and fulfilling. It was only after the Fall that thistles, thorns, and sweat came into the picture. Your task in the Kingdom is the toughest job you will ever love. While it may require much toil, it will also be a source of much joy. If lived right, the Kingdom life should not wear us out, stress us out, or burn us out. It is the rest we are to enter. Through it we learn to rest while working and to work while resting.

In 1982, two Russian cosmonauts returned from space having spent 211 days in orbit. Upon their return to earth, they suffered from dizziness, high pulse rates, and heart palpitations. They were unable to walk for a week and after a month were still undergoing therapy to strengthen weakened hearts and atrophied muscles. It was discovered that without the work of gravity pulling on their bodies, their muscles, including the heart, lost too much calcium and began to deteriorate.

Since that time, the Russians have prescribed a vigorous exercise program to counteract zero gravity. They invented a "penguin suit," which is a running suit laced with elastic bands. It resists the astronauts' every move, forcing them to exert strength and energy. In addition to a special diet, Russian cosmonauts also go through extensive workouts that include two-mile runs on a treadmill. Today, bone calcium loss is at a minimum for astronauts coming back home, making longer space journeys more of a possibility in the future.[6]

We all have thoughts of how wonderful it would be to live a life of ease, free from the gravity of everyday pressures. But truthfully, this kind of retirement only atrophies our faith and weakens the passions of our hearts. Our kingdom assignments are our penguin suits. They come equipped with resistance devices designed not to frustrate us but to strengthen us, so that one day we will arrive home in Christ having kept all unnecessary loss at a minimum.

Jesus knew agony and loss perhaps more than any person who has ever lived, yet His life taught us that only through great sacrifice do we find great satisfaction. Our pain now will be our joy then. Our trials only help us to fully appreciate the victory of our King.

The Kingdom of Heaven

The parable of the talents teaches us about working and reigning in the Kingdom of God. As the story goes, a man of great influence leaves on an extended trip, entrusting his estate to hired hands. In Luke's version, he is a king who gives a pound (or mina) of silver to each of his ten servants, instructing them to conduct business in his absence (see Luke 19:12-27). In Matthew's version, he is a lord who delegates five talents of gold to one servant, two to a second, and one to a third (see Matt. 25:14-30).

After many days, the master returns and calls them all to give an account of their activities. The first man was wise and more than doubled his investment. The master replies (paraphrased), "Well done, good and faithful servant. You are trustworthy. Because you have been faithful with this small amount, I am giving you authority over ten cities. Come be my partner." The second servant did likewise with his share and was rewarded with five cities.

The third, however, was careless with his portion. He merely dug a hole and buried the money. Approaching the king, he says, *"Master, I know you have high standards and hate careless ways, that you demand the best and make no allowances for error. I was afraid I might disappoint you, so I found a good hiding place and secured your money. Here it is, safe and sound down to the last cent"* (Matt. 25:24-25 The Message).

The king was furious, saying:

> *"You wicked servant!" the king roared. "Your own words condemn you. If you knew that I'm a hard man who takes what isn't mine and harvests crops I didn't plant, why didn't you deposit my money in the bank? At least I could have gotten some interest on it." Then, turning to the others standing nearby, the king ordered, "Take the money from this servant, and give it to the one who has ten pounds"* (Luke 19:22-24 NLT).

When questioned why the master was giving this man's portion to the most prosperous servant, he explains:

> *To those who use well what they have been given, even more will be given, and they will have an abundance. But from those who do nothing, even what little they have will be taken away* (Matt. 25:29 NLT).

Tending Your Talent

Earthly success is no guarantee of heavenly success. In the eyes of the world, success is passing the bar, making the grade, building a Fortune 500 company, breaking into the big leagues, gaining the respect of your peers, and retiring at a young age. It is having the right house, the right spouse, and the right jeans by Levi Strauss. If this is success, then most of us have failed miserably.

Thankfully, Heaven's dictionary defines success very differently. Success in life is how well we have devoted our lives to the service of the King. It is not *what* we have that counts but rather *how we invest* it. It is not how many servants we have, but rather how many people we have served. It is not how many fans we have, but whether God is a fan of our lifestyle. Success is fully cultivating our God-given talents in the Kingdom of God.

The measure of my ministry is not by how large our mailing list is, how many employees we have, or how much capital we own. It is the applause of Heaven. It is who I am and what I do when I am not on a stage in front of people. Similarly, your success in the Kingdom is not judged by the size of your congregation or how much Bible knowledge you dispense. It is how well you have loved those around you. We cannot afford to chase success at the expense of being obedient, and there is no need to covet it. If you do what you love and believe, success will come naturally.

The talents of this parable symbolize more than money. They represent all that we have been given—time, resources, intelligence, beauty, ability, family, and education. Some have more and some have less, but we are all responsible to steward what has been given to us. The wisest place any person can invest his or her gift of potential is with God.

If you are married, your marriage is a great place to start. When you tend to your relationship with your spouse, you are tending to your talent. My first job as a husband is to serve my wife. As I do, I not only invest in my marriage, but I also invest in the Kingdom of God.

When you love and discipline your children, you are tending to your talent. When you pray and cultivate your spiritual gifts, you are tending to your talent. We tend to our talent by honoring our parents and caring for them in their latter years. We tend to our talent when we are good stewards of our body. If you are an employer, tending to your talent is caring for and compensating your employees fairly and in a timely manner. If you own a business, it is managing your financial affairs with honesty, integrity, and generosity. If you are a leader in the church, it is serving others with diligence and reverence as unto the Lord.

Tending to your talent is being dutiful with your life, however great or small it is. When you cherish your portion, it demonstrates to God that you can be entrusted with more, and the way to contend for a future blessing is to be actively devoted to your current blessing. Those who are trustworthy with their own domain will ultimately be given dominion in the great domain.

This means that humbling yourself before your spouse advances the Kingdom. Making time for your children is time well spent. Praying for others is a privilege. Meditating on Scripture has great value. Giving to the poor holds eternal rewards. Being honest on your tax forms is joyous. Staying sexually pure is a precious gift.

Everyday Faithfulness

This parable paints a stark contrast between the faithful and the unfaithful. The difference between the unprofitable servant and the profitable servants was something as plain and everyday as faithfulness. The careless servant was fearful, lazy, insecure, and had a false concept of God, but most of all he was unfaithful. To the world, faithfulness is not very glamorous and is too ordinary to be noticed, but to the Lord it is too extraordinarily glorious to go unnoticed. Jesus indicates that faithfulness is more than merely a quality that leads to success. It is success!

The unfaithful servant was considered wicked because he did not value what the king had delegated to him. He treated his gift like trash. In the same way, how can we expect God to entrust us with something new when we don't appreciate what we already have? Why would He give us a bigger house or a nicer car when we don't take care of the one we currently own? You say you need a new job, but are you grateful for the one He has already given you? Your church or anointing may not be what you have been praying for, but do you faithfully serve the one you do have?

God's definition of faithfulness is more than just gritting our teeth and holding the line. Jesus defines faithfulness as increase. Our talents are not just there to be protected. They are made to multiply. Growth is your responsibility, not God's. The way to maintain the ground we already have taken is to keep taking ground. When the two servants multiplied what they had been entrusted with, they were rewarded with more.

There is a story told about a veteran missionary couple returning home from Africa after many years of service. They left the mission field discouraged, defeated, and afraid. Their health was deteriorating, and they had no retirement money to fall back on. They learned that President Teddy Roosevelt, returning from a hunting expedition, happened to be booked on the same ship as they were.

When they docked in New York City, there was much fanfare given to the president's arrival. Dignitaries and members of the media were there waiting for him, and passengers fought to catch a glimpse of the president. Meanwhile, the missionary couple slipped off the ship and quietly walked past the entourage, unnoticed and unappreciated.

That night, the husband confessed to his wife that he was harboring bitter feelings for the president. He was upset that a crowd of important people were there to celebrate the president as he came home and that there was no one there to celebrate their homecoming. After all, they had given their lives in faithful service to God all these years. His wife told him to take it up with the Lord, and so he did. As he prayed about how unfair their reception was compared to the president's, the Lord tenderly said, "But you're not home yet." [7]

There are rewards for remaining faithful to the Lord in this life, but they may not always be realized in this lifetime. *"Let us not grow weary while doing good, for in due season we shall reap if we do not lose heart"* (Gal. 6:9). Someday there will be a homecoming for you, and on that day your faithfulness and obedience will be celebrated.

Authority for Cities

When Adam and Eve fell, they did not fall from Heaven; they fell from their dominion. Dominion is an important concept in the Kingdom, because it is related to our domain. We are not just inheriting land but a sphere of authority. Jesus successfully reclaimed dominion over the earth, and it is through the Kingdom that He restores this authority to us.

When the king rewarded the first two servants, he granted them authority over cities. I contend that the cities Christ will entrust to the faithful are not heavenly cities, but actual, literal cities here on earth—London, Beijing, Las Vegas, New Delhi, Nairobi, St. Petersburg, Rio de Janeiro, Mexico City. Notice the servants didn't have to take the cities. The king already owned them. The season for God's release of city authority is fast approaching. He will reward the faithful with the honor of reigning with Him, for Christ entrusts cities to those who have diligently served their post.

Conclusion

God's Kingdom is a paradise world simply because Christ rules this world, and we are standing at the threshold of the greatest adventure of our lives. The Lord is offering us the opportunity of a lifetime, and when the opportunity of a lifetime comes we must be sure to act within the lifetime of that opportunity. The Kingdom needs us as much as we need the Kingdom, and only it can offer what our souls truly crave—a vision and a pursuit.

So go ahead. Venture out into uncharted territory. Run uninhibited through the jungle sanctuary of your call. Scuffle with enormous spiders for the lost of your city. Fight off wild boars to protect your family and your marriage. Don't be satisfied until you reach the crest of your promised land. You have a land to conquer, an adventure to live, and a Kingdom to advance. We now have a Kingdom to live for and a cause to die for.

Endnotes

1. Joseph Thayer, *The Online Bible Thayer's Greek Lexicon* (Ontario, Canada: Woodside Bible Fellowship, 1993).

2. C.F. Keil and F. Delitzsch, *Keil and Delitzsch Commentary on the Old Testament*, vol. 1 (Grand Rapids, MI: Eerdman's Publishing Company, 1980), 90.

3. http://thinkexist.com/quotation/a_man_who_works_with_his_ hands_ is_a_laborer-a_man/181851.html, accessed April 30, 2009.

4. John L. Mason, *An Enemy Called Average* (Insight Publishing Group: Tulsa, OK, 1990), 55.

5. Roy B. Zuck, *The Speaker's Quote Book* (Kregal Publications: Grand Rapids, MI, 1997), 416.

6.   Craig Brian Larson, *Illustrations For Preaching & Teaching* (Baker
     Books: Grand Rapids, MI, 1997) 60; http://www.time.com/time/
     magazine/article/0,9171,966567,00.html?iid=chix-sphere (accessed
     May 3, 2009).

7.   Larson, *Illustrations For Preaching & Teaching*, 197-198.

CHAPTER 14

CROWN OF AUTHORITY, CROWN OF GLORY

"...made us kings and priests to our God; and we shall reign on the earth."
(Revelation 5:10)

T HE story of Jack and Jill is more than a cute nursery rhyme. The poem was first published in 1795 and is said to recount the gruesome beheading of King Louis XVI and Queen Marie Antoinette during the French Revolution.[1] In light of this fact, it doesn't seem like a very fitting story for children. Be that as it may, the tragedy of Jack and Jill is much like poor Humpty Dumpty's—all had a great fall.

> Jack and Jill went up a hill to fetch a pail of water.
> Jack fell down and broke his crown,
> and Jill came tumbling after.

The unfortunate thing is that Jack's fall predicated Jill's demise. In the same way, the tragedy of the story of Adam and Eve is that Adam's fall predicated the fall of humankind. He lost his head; or said another way—Adam lost his headship of authority, and when our forefather relinquished his kingly crown to the devil, so did we.

But where the first Adam failed, the Last Adam succeeded. Adam lived in a perfect world and sinned, but Jesus remained sinless in an imperfect world. The first Adam was *made* in the image of God and lost it; the Last Adam *is* the very image of God and restored it. Adam submitted to satan's voice in the Garden of Eden, but Jesus resisted satan's voice in the Garden of Gethsemane. Adam's demise was that he disobeyed God's command, but the triumph of the Messiah was that He did only what His Father commanded Him to do. Jesus now replaces Adam as our spiritual forefather.

Adam and Eve were born to lead. When God said, *"Let them have dominion,"* He would not undermine their authority to rule. Their dominion became an irrevocable and unchangeable law, so final that they had the ability to give it away. But because they had no authority to eat the forbidden fruit, they surrendered the authority which they already possessed. When Jesus said, *"Behold, I give you the authority,"* He was restoring what Adam lost (see Luke 10:19). In Christ we are now born-again leaders.

> For since by man came death, by Man also came the resurrection of the dead. For as in Adam all die, even so in Christ all shall be made alive. ...The first man Adam became a living being. The last Adam became a life-giving Spirit (1 Corinthians 15:21-22,45).

Jesus Christ is called the Last Adam, because He became the prototype for a new way to be human. Through Adam's disobedience death came to the human race, but through Christ's obedience death was overcome. Jesus overcame sin, demonstrating that it is possible to live a life governed by the Spirit of God. We have now been crowned with His resurrection life.

Because He conquered sin and death, Christ's dominion is superior to Adam's. Adam was only given dominion over the earth, but Jesus has been given dominion over the heavens and the earth. What the Father restored to us was neither the old nor even the original but went even further in Christ. He allows us to share in the inheritance of His Son's reign. Through Christ, God instituted a greater law through a stronger covenant. God not only intends for Christ to rule, but He also chooses us as His ruling partners. By redeeming us from sin, we are now liberated to be capable of judging the nations with equity, righteousness, and justice (see Rev. 2:26-27). This is the Kingdom of God.

Kingdom of Priests

When God birthed the nation of Israel, He installed a kingdom unlike any institution on earth. It was more than a monarchy; it was a theocracy. Yahweh Himself was Israel's King.

But this form of government did not last long. During the time of the prophet Samuel, the people wanted a king like the surrounding nations. The elders demanded of Samuel, *"Give us a king"* (see 1 Sam. 8:5 NLT). The Lord God responded to their demands, instructing Samuel, *"Do everything they say to you...for it is Me they are rejecting, not you. They don't want Me to be their king any longer"* (1 Sam. 8:7 NLT).

> *...He will take your sons and appoint them for his own chariots and to be his horsemen, and some will run before his chariots. He will...set some to plow his ground and reap his harvest... He will take your daughters to be perfumers, cooks, and bakers. And he will take the best of your fields, your vineyards, and your olive groves, and give them to his servants. He will take a tenth of your grain and your vintage, and give it to his officers and servants. And he will take your male servants, your female servants, your finest young men, and your donkeys, and put them to his work. He will take a tenth of your sheep. And you will be his servants. (1 Sam. 8:11-17).*

God here proceeded to forewarn the people about the nature of kings, but the people insisted on being ruled by a man, so God gave them Saul.

I believe God intended to establish the Kingdom of Heaven through Jacob's children, but the people refused, rejecting the Enthroned One as their King. They wanted *a* king to rule them rather than *the* King.

Israel missed out on an historic opportunity to be the only nation on the planet to embody the Kingdom of God. Since that time, no government on earth has ever been under the direct leadership of Heaven.

The Israelites misdirected God's promise to Abraham (see Gen. 12:2-3). They made themselves the object of the promise instead of a conduit for it. Israel was called to inspire and influence the world but instead were inspired and influenced *by* the world. They were to reign over the nations, not become subject to them (see Deut. 15:6). They assumed God would save them through a worldly king instead of saving the world through their King. Jehovah's plan of salvation was much bigger than the vision of Israel's elders.

But before we go pointing fingers, western Christianity is in danger of falling into a similar trap. We have become so self-absorbed, introspective, and consumer-driven that we are in danger of losing sight of our mission and our King. We have traded our influence for affluence. We have settled for the message of personal salvation instead of the message of the planet's salvation. We stop at being blessed instead of being a blessing.

We have allowed ourselves to be inspired by the way the world operates, incorporating their methods as our own. It seems our communities of faith are rapidly becoming less communal and more like big business. Most churches conduct business meetings, hold interviews for pastoral vacancies, poll members regarding policy change, and vote on those holding office. We have employees, boards, titles, clients, salaries, mortgages, organizational hierarchies, CEOs, and 401Ks.

If corporations create vision statements, we feel we should. If companies carry debt, so must we. If managers play hardball, so do we. We have borrowed from how the business sector functions and plugged it into our churches, but the problem is corporate America is a poor model for a Kingdom community. Let us take heed, lest we fall into Israel's same errors.

Not a Democracy

For all intents and purposes, the people of God are to be a theocracy—a Heaven-ruled monarchy. We are priests, and Christ is our High Priest. Unlike Israel's elders, our vote and opinion do not matter in the grand scheme of things.

Democracy has taught us that it is patriotic to openly criticize our leaders, that we have the right to disrespect authority. Whether a president, prime minister, or political figure, if we disagree with their policies we are not ashamed to publicly ridicule them. In fact, our society seems to applaud such denigration, priding ourselves on free speech.

While this may be how the world operates, it is not how a kingdom does. Kings rule by inheritance and conquest, not by election. A king does not give anyone the right to question his judgment. His word is the final say on a matter. What he decides is law. What he declares is truth. He owns everything within his domain, including the opinions of the people.

We enter the danger zone when we begin disrespecting our leaders, spiritual or civic. There is a fine line between evaluating leadership and unrighteously judging it. We should respect those whom God has placed in authority over us whether they have earned it or not. We honor our leaders not because of their track record or their stance on an issue, but simply out of submission to God. If we cannot honor the leaders whom we can see, how can we honor the One whom we cannot see?

The power of establishing policy has not been delegated to us. That is the responsibility of our King. Our objective is merely to make known His laws to the people. This is what qualifies us to reign with Christ. The call of Israel is also our call—to present the world with its King.

For King and Country

"Ask not what your country can do for you. Ask what you can do for your country."

—John F. Kennedy

Those who are great in the Kingdom of God don't ask what the Kingdom can do for them; they ask what they can do for the King. Authority in God's Kingdom is given to those who serve well, and according to Jesus a slave makes the best kind of leader (see Mark 10:42-45).

Some people live their lives with a gross sense of entitlement. When driving, it's their lane; when parking, it's their spot; when violated, it's their right; when injured, it's their claim. As Americans, we are taught that we have certain rights that are inalienable and inherent. We make laws to protect our Bill of Rights, because we live in world that is not governed by the law of love.

At times, we act as though the government owes us something in return for our pain. We expect the system to come to our rescue and pay for our inconvenience in times of injustice, war, or natural disaster. When this doesn't happen we too quickly blame our government for being prejudiced or inept. While this behavior may be accepted in our culture, there is no room for this kind of attitude in the Kingdom.

During our last visit to China, Meljoné and I sat down with a pastor who spent over 20 years of his life in prison for the gospel. He was incarcerated on two occasions. During that time, however, his underground church grew exponentially. What struck me most about this man was that, even at the age of 77, he was perhaps the most joyful and energetic man I have ever met. There appeared not even a hint of bitterness toward the government or the Lord for his injustice. During our covert visit, he served us like kings, wept when he talked about Christ, and lavished us with many books and prophecies he wrote while in prison.

Even though his wife had died while he was in prison, he had a glimmer in his eyes as he talked about prison life, as if it were a great honor to suffer for the Lord. He said that the Chinese believers don't take a young man called to ministry seriously until he has spent time in prison for the gospel. Imagine that. Their most trusted spiritual leaders are all ex-cons!

He was quick to credit persecution as a key to the estimated 30,000 people coming to Christ daily in China. We also learned from him that the Chinese believers feel a strong call to bring the gospel to the Muslim nations of the Middle East. The Chinese are not intimidated by persecution. They feel that the persecution they have had to endure under communism is good preparation for the persecution they must endure in the Middle East.

We westerners can learn a lot from our eastern brothers and sisters. Namely, that the Kingdom does not exist to serve our interests, but rather we are here to serve the Kingdom's. We are not brought in to assert our claims or to claim our rights. Our rights, even our right to freedom, have been crucified on the Cross of Christ. Our only claim is our claim on God's mercy based on the shed blood of Jesus.

Having authority is not an entitlement. It is an honor. Since all authority is established by God, even our authority belongs to Him. People who harp on authority only prove they have none.

Our Responsibility is our Authority

And I bestow upon you a kingdom, just as My Father bestowed one upon Me, that you may eat and drink at My table in My kingdom, and sit on thrones judging the twelve tribes of Israel (Luke 22:29-30).

I've always been uncomfortable when believers speak of the crown they will possess in Heaven. What arrogance! We surely won't be wearing crowns in Heaven, I thought. Shouldn't we boast of the manifold crowns that Christ Jesus will be wearing? After all, the elders cast down their crowns before the throne as they worship (see Rev. 4:10).

But as it turns out, I am the arrogant one. I was humbled to discover that a crown awaits those who victoriously inherit the Kingdom of God. The Bible speaks of the crown of righteousness given to all who cherish the appearing of the righteous Judge (see 2 Tim. 4:8). Paul mentions an imperishable crown that awaits those who run the race well (see 1 Cor. 9:25). James speaks of the crown of life that is granted to those who endure temptation, love the Lord, and gain His approval (see James

1:12). Christ adds that this crown belongs to those who are faithful in tribulation (see Rev. 2:10).

This is wonderful, but all these crowns seem to be reserved for the millennial Kingdom. Is there a crown available in the present Kingdom? Yes. Jesus exhorted the church of Philadelphia not to let anyone take their crown, which implies that there *is* a crown obtainable to us in this age (see Rev. 3:11). We are not to lay this one down just yet, because it is the crown of our authority.

In the Hebrew Scriptures, the priests were given a crown to wear. It represented honor, holiness, and spiritual authority. Today, this crown of authority is available to those entering the Kingdom of Heaven. As the royal priesthood of God, we are to the Kingdom what the priests were to Israel (see 1 Pet. 2:9; Exod. 19:5-6; Rev. 1:6; 5:10). Just as they stood before the people to represent God, we stand before God and represent Him to our world. Our crown is not a right. It is a cherished responsibility.

The Three Arenas

There are three strategic arenas in which God has given you a crown of authority, and it is here where we all can exercise spiritual responsibility. These three are: the Kingdom, the church, and the home. Their importance cannot be understated. Without the arena of the Kingdom, we gain no opportunity for greatness. Without the arena of the church, we train no community of leaders. Without the arena of the home, we leave no legacy for our children.

Christ is the central figure and chief authority of each arena. He is the King of the Kingdom, the Head of the church, and the Master of the home (see Matt. 21:4-5; John 18:36-37; Eph. 5:23; Col. 1:18; Mark 13:35; and Col. 4:1). To the level He dominates these three areas is the level that we are granted authority to rule with Him. Let's examine them a little closer.

The Kingdom

Where there is a kingdom there is authority to rule, and the Kingdom of God is our opportunity for greatness. Surprisingly, however, greatness in the Kingdom is reserved for the simplest among us. Jesus never pandered to the wealthy or the sophisticated. He often spoke to the simple and poor in heart, and there is none more unpretentious among us than our children.

My children continually teach me a lot about the Kingdom. Once, I was changing a heater filter in our house when the stepstool I was standing on collapsed. Instantly, I had a headache, and pain shot through my left wrist. My wife and 2-year-old heard a crash and came out of the bedroom. Seeing me lay there in the hallway next to the broken stepstool, Meljoné asked if I was okay. I said, "I think so, but my wrist is killing me."

Soraya could sense I was in pain, so she came up and gave me a big hug. Meljoné suggested they pray for Daddy, so Soraya placed her hand on my head, closed her eyes, and said, "Healed." Amazingly, all the pain left in my wrist. In fact, it felt better than it was before the accident.

In life, we all must pass through a season of childhood, and in the Kingdom it is no different. Childlike faith is a rite of passage and is highly honored in God's economy. Jesus thinks of greatness in terms of the humility of a child. Not only do children hold rank in the Kingdom of Heaven, but the Kingdom belongs to them.

> *...Unless you are converted and become as little children, you will by no means enter the kingdom of Heaven. Therefore whoever humbles himself as this little child is the greatest in the kingdom of Heaven* (Matthew 18:3-4).

> *...Let the little children come to Me, and do not forbid them; for of such is the Kingdom of God* (Luke 18:16).

The Kingdom of God is a kid-friendly culture closer to that of a kindergarten than a graduate school. It is not for the high and lofty but the low and humble. Pride caused the first fall, so to enter into what was lost we must act in the opposite spirit.

Childlike, Not Childish

Children have a way of changing the atmosphere of a room. Their honesty can be brutal yet refreshing. Their humility is attractive and unsurpassed. They can be as stubborn as a mule yet innocent as a lamb. Children have the unique ability to believe the unbelievable, forgive the unforgivable, and lighten up a moment. A child who displays genuine sincerity, compassion, and dependence is both stimulating and inspiring.

However, let us not confuse childlikeness with childishness. They are as unalike as earwigs and earwax. Childish behavior is self-serving. It is my cup, my toy, and my bike. It exhibits infantile and tantrum-throwing behavior. It is immature and self-absorbed. A child who is shown only conditional love and is never disciplined becomes an insecure adult plagued with a sense of entitlement, always grabbing for more and trying to protect what is theirs. There are many childish parents *and* Christians today.

Childlikeness, however, possesses trust and faithfulness. It is bold, mature, and courageous. It displays the true fruit of the Spirit—genuine affection, contagious joy, transcendent peace, patient fortitude, moral excellence, benevolent virtue, tender compassion, unwavering fidelity, and radical self-control. In the Kingdom, childlikeness leads to prominence, but childishness is intolerable and unacceptable.

> *Whoever therefore breaks one of the least of these command-*
> *ments, and teaches men so, shall be called least in the king-*
> *dom of Heaven; but whoever does and teaches them, he shall*
> *be called great in the kingdom of Heaven* (Matthew 5:19).

Jesus teaches that there will be some who are great and some who are least in the Kingdom of Heaven, implying that God has given each of us an opportunity to be great in His Kingdom. Greatness with God is more about availability than ability. You don't have to be wealthy, talented, clever, charming, cute, or articulate to be great in the Kingdom. It just takes humble obedience. This invitation is open to all—the poor and the rich, the popular and the outcast, the smart and the uneducated, the privileged and the underprivileged. Essentially, we are as great in the Kingdom as we choose to be.

The theological approach to reading God's Word, the intellectual approach to evangelism, and the academic approach to hearing God's voice all pale in comparison to the childlike approach. Childlikeness reads and believes, listens and obeys, and speaks the truth in love. The childlike approach to life is simply more effective and more pleasing to the Lord.

In our campus ministry, we had a student in our fellowship who was very much like a child. He was sweet, sincere, and affectionate but socially immature. He had a genuine heart of love for Christ and for people, but his hygiene challenges and quirky mannerisms scared off would-be friends. But would you know that he was our most effective soul-winner? He was not afraid to share his faith with the *whosoevers* of the world. He led athletes, fraternity guys, and some of the most influential people on campus to Christ and to our fellowship.

When I was in Argentina, we were told that God was using 5- and 6-year-olds to extend the revival. These kindergartners were traveling from house to house asking if anyone was sick and in need of prayer. As they laid hands on them, people would fall under the power and get up healed. Their bold faith attracted the power of God, and their unpretentious compassion disarmed the skeptical.

Children become great in God's eyes when they simply obey, and to enter the Kingdom we must be like them. The more we become as they are, the more we become as Christ is, and the more Christ reigns in us, the more He can reign through us. We can learn a lot from a preschooler.

The Church

We are not called to just attend church. We are called to be the church, yet Christ only referenced the church on three occasions. For every one passage in which He mentions the church, there are almost 30 others about the kingdom. He first referred to the church in Matthew 18 when giving instructions about a brother in sin. The second is in Revelation 2 and 3 when He addresses the seven churches of Asia Minor. The third is found in Matthew 16. Here He also remarks about the kingdom, so let's review this one.

> *...you are Peter, and on this rock I will build My church, and the gates of Hades shall not prevail against it. And I will give you the keys of the kingdom of Heaven, and whatever you bind on earth will be bound in Heaven, and whatever you loose on earth will be loosed in Heaven* (Matthew 16:18-19).

According to this verse, the Kingdom and the church are not the same entity. They are similar but distinct. The church belongs to Christ and is being built by Him; the Kingdom, however, is firmly established upon an unshakable throne (see Ps. 93:2; 103:19). Whereas the church is a community of people coming out of the world, the Kingdom is a company of people invading the world. If the church is our position, then the Kingdom is our inheritance.

> *..."Come, I will show you the bride, the Lamb's wife." And he carried me away in the Spirit to a great and high mountain, and showed me the great city, the holy Jerusalem, descending out of Heaven from God* (Revelation 21:9-10).

In Scripture, the church is depicted as a body, a building, an army, an athlete, and a bride. This bride is evolving into a spiritual city known as the New Jerusalem. Members of the Body of Christ are not so much those who attend church meetings but those who hold citizenship papers in Zion. This New Jerusalem is the capital city of the Kingdom and will serve as the center of the world in the age to come. It is a city that literally comes out of Heaven. While this great city is the heart of the Kingdom, the Kingdom itself extends well beyond its gates.

The church is not a physical building. It is the people, and they are becoming the earthly headquarters of God. Buildings have value, but they can't guarantee that our churches will grow or assure that the Kingdom will advance. For the sake of illustration, if the building is the church, the property is the Kingdom. The building is the key structure on the real estate, but the property encompasses more than just the building. In the same way, the church is being built upon the Kingdom. It is not the only expression of the Kingdom, but the central one.

What happens to a church is important to the Lord just as what happens to a wife is important to her husband, but what happens to the Kingdom through the church is equally important. A church body must never lose sight of the Kingdom when in transition, when making decisions, or in the work of evangelism. A pastor must not think that he is called only to his church, and an evangelist must not think that he is called only to populate the Kingdom. Together they should be working to build up both (see Acts 28:23-31; Eph. 4:11-12).

The Gate and the Door

Jesus declared that upon Peter's confession He would build His church. Peter professed, *"You are the Christ, the Son of the Living God,"* and this revelation is the foundation of the church (Matt. 16:16). The church today is still founded upon Peter's declaration, for this confession is the very heart and soul of our theology.

Jesus added that "the gates of hades shall not prevail against it." Fortified cities in ancient times used the gates of the city to conduct business and hold councils, and they were places of impenetrable strength. Christ is saying that the plots, strategies, and strength of the evil one can never prevail against the truth that He is the Christ, the Son of the Living God. We should not be intimidated by the gates of hell, for the gate of hell is also the door of the church—it just matters which direction one is traveling.

In the days of Elijah, Eliakim was overseer of the household of King Hezekiah. It is said that he carried a heavy key on a loop slung over his shoulder, giving him the power to grant or deny others access to the king. That key represented Eliakim's full administrative authority in the kingdom. Similarly, the church carries with it a heavy key. We have the power to grant people access to the presence of God. The Lord has given us full administrative authority in His Kingdom and given us an audience with the King of kings.[2] (See 2 Kings 18:18, 19:2, Is. 22:20-23.)

Jesus states that His Kingdom has keys, and He gave the keys of the Kingdom to Peter first, then to the rest of the apostles. (See Matt. 16:19, 18:18.) Peter used these keys to make known the gospel to the Jews on the day of Pentecost and to the Gentiles at the house of Cornelius. He received these keys first because he confessed Christ first.

Keys do two things. They keep things out, and they let things in.

Keys represent authority. When God told Abraham He would make him into a great nation, He was establishing Kingdom rule, but when He promised him a great name He was establishing Kingdom authority. Those justified by faith in Christ also come into the promise of Abraham—Kingdom rule and Kingdom authority.

With any authority comes accountability. The current keys that God has given you are on loan from Heaven. God is permitting you to test drive Kingdom authority to determine if you are responsible enough to own that place of dominion in the age to come. If you will take your job assignment seriously, God will give you these keys permanently and perhaps even more.

Keys also represent nobility. When a city wants to honor a hero, they give the upstanding citizen a key to the city. Similarly, we have been given an honored key to our Father's prized possession—the Heavenly City of the Kingdom of God. This is the church of the Kingdom.

A Kingdom of Color

Our responsibility to the community of Christ is vital to our development in Christ. Rick Warren writes, "While your relationship to Christ is personal, God never intends it to be private."[3] Whereas the Kingdom of God is our occupation, the church is our identity. To disregard each other is to disrespect ourselves and our Maker.

Think of the church as a vast forest filled with redwoods, firs, maples, pines, evergreens, and every type of tree known on the earth. We are diverse, representing every culture and nation on earth, and God loves our diversity. Despite a popular bumper sticker stating otherwise, God is *not* colorblind.[4] He created the different colors and ethnicities, and He takes delight in their uniqueness. Though we are unique, we all share the same DNA underground. Our roots stem not from Africa, China, or Europe but from one righteous Seed.

I recently read that botanists have identified an unknown fungus that helps reduce competition among tree roots when they touch each other. This organism is able to link the roots of different trees together, even trees of dissimilar species. In this way, whole forests can be linked together like an underground network, helping one another survive. If one portion of the forest receives more direct sunlight, the whole forest does. If one section has access to water, all have access. If one tree absorbs nutrients, they all do.

This is a picture of the church. Above ground we are a colorful kingdom drawing out the God-colors of this world, but underground we are oaks of righteousness linked together by the unity of the Spirit. We must rely on each other for survival. You need us, and we need you, and there is no need for competition. Your success in the Lord is our success. Our victory is your victory. My breakthrough is your breakthrough. The key is to allow our roots to touch each other.

The church community my wife and I enjoy is committed to being in covenant relationship with each other. This means that we have decided to love one another through the good, the bad, and the ugly. We are learning how to honor each other, and as we do we open our lives up to one another. This is how trust gets built, and it is this trust that sustains us. When I need to be challenged or rebuked by the elders, I don't feel cornered or the need to run away, because I trust their love for me. It is not always all chocolate and roses. We still experience our fair share of conflict, but no longer do we feel the need to avoid it. Conflict is evidence that we are being authentically real and is an invitation for deeper intimacy.

Christ commands us to love one another. As ministers, we must be careful not to use God's people as free labor for the activities of our church or ministry. They are not here to serve us—we are here to serve them. We err when we make the church building or the church meeting more important than the church people.

The Home

The kingdom of the home carries more spiritual authority than we have presumed. The local church deserves our steadfast attention but not to the neglect of our families. Since the house of God is more spiritual than physical, the home should serve as a God's sanctuary just as much as the church does.

The early church was not nearly as organized as the modern church, but they were able to successfully sustain revival. On the day of Pentecost, they assimilated three thousand converts into the church. How did 120 people disciple 3,000? It is because the Jewish men of that time were accustomed to functioning as priests of their home. Each Sabbath the head of the house would lead their family and guests in prayers, meals, blessings, readings, and *midrash*. They were home group leaders and spiritual elders. The 3,000 converts were simply folded into these organic cell groups.

The upper room experience teaches that an outpouring of the Spirit will never fulfill its purpose if only confined to a church building. It must pour out onto the streets, impacting our homes, marriages, children, and neighborhoods. This is how we "pastor" revival—by not making the revival meeting the focus of the revival. Revivals don't begin by people seeking revival. They begin when people seek the Lord. Our focus is always Christ, and when His will prevails where we live and work, revival will be sustained. Charles Spurgeon said, "The light that shines the furthest shines brightest at home."

Indecent Exposure

When Meljoné and I were newlyweds, a famous minister was holding a one-night event at a hotel near us. The flyer advertised a night of miracles with a world-renowned apostle. Someone gave us some tickets, so we decided to go.

As the music began, the crowd sang and danced with great enthusiasm. In fact, it was borderline pandemonium. I had no problem with this whatsoever. I love loud expressions of love for the Lord, and I have had my fair share of outrageous outbreaks of praise. The problem was that I felt the polar opposite on the inside. My spirit seemed awkwardly cold and detached.

Naturally, I thought there was something wrong with me. I tried to press through and focus on Christ, but something was amiss. I hoped that it would get better, but it only got worse.

After a long media presentation that puffed up the minister and his international humanitarian efforts, the apostle gave an even longer plea for money. The offering portion of the meeting lasted for almost an hour, and I was having an inner battle. I was grieved, upset, and felt emotionally manipulated. I wanted to leave, but I didn't want to prevent Meljoné from missing out on something good from the meeting.

Fifty-five minutes into the pre-offering sermon, the Holy Spirit spoke to me and said, "You are responsible for what you expose your wife to." At that, I grabbed her hand and walked out. Believe it or not, the minister tried to pronounce a curse over us as he saw us leaving.

That night I learned a valuable principle. I am responsible for what happens under my watch, and I will be either judged or rewarded for what I allow to take place under my authority. I must choose carefully what I expose my family to, for they will eventually imitate what I tolerate. What I do in moderation, my children will do in excess.

Before we can be kings in the marketplace and priests in the church, we must be kings and priests in our own homes. The Kingdom of God should not only dominate our churches, but it must also monopolize our households.

We are guilty of relying too heavily on the church to spoon-feed our spirits, mentor our children, give us a place to serve, and bring us into the presence of God. When we place the priesthood of the pastor above the priesthood of the home, our neediness and poor leadership will eventually drag down the church. However, if we lead our homes by praying with our spouses, discipling our children, honoring the Sabbath, and hosting the Holy Spirit, we will only take the church higher.

Crown of Glory

Shepherd the flock...serving as overseers, not by compulsion but willingly, not for dishonest gain but eagerly; not as being lords over those entrusted to you, but being examples to the flock; and when the Chief Shepherd appears, you will receive a crown of glory that does not fade away (1 Peter 5:2-4).

A bright future awaits those who genuinely love and diligently care for the people whom God has given them authority to lead. Peter calls it a crown of glory, and this glory is the zenith of our Kingdom experience.

We talk a lot about original sin, but not enough is said about original glory. Genesis 3 recounts original sin, but Genesis 1 is original glory, and before there was ever sin there was glory. The story of humankind does not begin with sin but with glory; neither will it end with sin but with glory.

If we endure, we shall also reign with Him...(2 Timothy 2:12).

One of the many rewards for those who endure tribulation is inheriting the Kingdom of Heaven and reigning with Christ in the next age. Our life in Christ now is merely training for reigning; it is the school where we learn to rule. Endurance is more than keeping the faith or resisting temptation. It is to remain standing after everyone else has collapsed. William Barclay wrote, "Endurance is not just the ability to bear a hard thing, but to turn it into glory."[5]

God has a brilliant plan for your life. It is called His glory, and inheriting the Kingdom will be the crowning moment of your life.

Conclusion

The goal of your life in the Kingdom is to hear Christ say to you, *"Well done, good and faithful servant"* (Matt. 25:21). These words are reserved for those who have successfully and victoriously overcome the world. More important than the score of the big game is the score we will receive on that day.

The "well done" of God is the ultimate *welcome mat* of Heaven. So welcome to the eternal Kingdom of God. Welcome to God's paradise. Welcome to a life lived inside the gates, outside the lines, above the rim, under the radar, and over the rainbow. It is a reality just beyond the horizon where impossibilities are possible and improbabilities are certain. It is an unshakable journey where enemies find reconciliation, broken homes find restoration, and lonely hearts find fascination.

Endnotes

1. "Jack and Jill poem," Nursery Rhymes lyrics, origins and history, http://www.rhymes.org.uk/jack_and_jill.htm (accessed April 04, 2009); "Jack and Jill," Famous quotes, http://www.famousquotes .me.uk/nursery_rhymes/jack_and_jill.htm (accessed April 04, 2009).

2. Chuck Missler, *Notes on the Book of Revelation*, 86.

3. Rick Warren, *The Purpose Driven Life* (Grand Rapids, MI: Zondervan, 2002), 130.

4. The bumper sticker reads "God Is Colorblind."

5. Roy B. Zuck, *The Speaker's Quote Book* (Kregal Publications: Grand Rapids, MI, 1997), 129.

KINGDOM VERSES
FOR MEDITATION

his Kingdom odyssey began for me when I read John 15:7 and determined to daily abide in the words of Christ. Starting with the book of Mark and continuing through the gospels, I purposed to meditate only on the words of Christ throughout my day. What I quickly realized was that the Kingdom of God dominated the teachings and conversations of Christ. May I encourage you to do likewise? As you do, may this Kingdom paradigm revolutionize you too. An adequate list of Scripture verses concerning the Kingdom can be found below for meditation.

Hebrew Scriptures

Genesis 1:26-28—*"Then God said, 'Let Us make man in Our image, according to Our likeness; let them have dominion over the fish of the sea, over the birds of the air, and over the cattle, over all the earth and over every creeping thing that creeps on the earth.' So God created man in His own image; in the image of God He* created him; male and female He created them. Then God blessed them, and God said to them, 'Be fruitful and multiply; fill the earth and subdue it; have dominion over the fish of the sea, over the birds of the air, and over every living thing that moves on the earth.'"

Exodus 19:6—"'And you shall be to Me a kingdom of priests and a holy nation.' These are the words which you shall speak to the children of Israel."

Numbers 24:7—"...His kingdom shall be exalted."

Numbers 24:17-19—"I see Him, but not now; I behold Him, but not near; a Star shall come out of Jacob; a Scepter shall rise out of Israel, and batter the brow of Moab, and destroy all the sons of tumult. And Edom shall be a possession; Seir also, his enemies, shall be a possession, while Israel does valiantly. Out of Jacob One shall have dominion, and destroy the remains of the city."

2 Samuel 7:12-16—"When your days are fulfilled and you rest with your fathers, I will set up your seed after you, who will come from your body, and I will establish his kingdom. He shall build a house for My Name, and I will establish the throne of his kingdom forever. I will be his Father, and he shall be My son. If he commits iniquity, I will chasten him with the rod of men and with the blows of the sons of men. But My mercy shall not depart from him, as I took it from Saul, whom I removed from before you. And your house and your kingdom shall be established forever before you. Your throne shall be established forever."

1 Kings 9:5—"Then I will establish the throne of your kingdom over Israel forever, as I promised David your father, saying, 'You shall not fail to have a man on the throne of Israel.'"

1 Chronicles 17:11-14—*"And it shall be, when your days are fulfilled, when you must go to be with your fathers, that I will set up your seed after you, who will be of your sons; and I will establish his kingdom. He shall build Me a house, and I will establish his throne forever. I will be his Father, and he shall be My son; and I will not take My mercy away from him, as I took it from him who was before you. And I will establish him in My house and in My kingdom forever; and his throne shall be established forever."*

1 Chronicles 22:10—*"He shall build a house for My Name, and he shall be My son, and I will be his Father; and I will establish the throne of his kingdom over Israel forever."*

1 Chronicles 29:11—*"Yours, O Lord, is the greatness, the power and the glory, the victory and the majesty; for all that is in Heaven and in earth is Yours; Yours is the kingdom, O Lord, and You are exalted as head over all."*

Job 25:2—*"Dominion and fear belong to Him; He makes peace in His high places."*

Job 38:33—*"Do you know the ordinances of the heavens? Can you set their dominion over the earth?"*

Psalm 2:6-8—*"Yet I have set My King on My holy hill of Zion. I will declare the decree: the Lord has said to Me, 'You are My Son, today I have begotten You. Ask of Me, and I will give You the nations for Your inheritance, and the ends of the earth for Your possession."*

Psalm 5:2—*"Give heed to the voice of my cry, my King and my God, for to You I will pray."*

Psalm 8:4-6—*"What is man that You are mindful of him, and the son of man that You visit him? For You have made him a little lower than the angels, and You have crowned him with glory and honor. You have made him to have dominion over the works of Your hands; you have put all things under his feet."*

Psalm 10:16—*"The Lord is King forever and ever; the nations have perished out of His land."*

Psalm 20:9—*"Save, Lord! May the King answer us when we call."*

Psalm 22:27-29—*"All the ends of the world shall remember and turn to the Lord, and all the families of the nations shall worship before You. For the kingdom is the Lord's, and He rules over the nations. All the prosperous of the earth shall eat and worship; all those who go down to the dust shall bow before Him, even he who cannot keep himself alive."*

Psalm 24:8-10—*"Who is this King of glory? The Lord strong and mighty, the Lord mighty in battle. Lift up your heads, O you gates! Lift up, you everlasting doors! And the King of glory shall come in. Who is this King of glory? The Lord of hosts, he is the King of glory."*

Psalm 29:10—*"The Lord sat enthroned at the Flood, and the Lord sits as King forever."*

Psalm 44:4—*"You are my King, O God; command victories for Jacob."*

Psalm 45:1,6—*"My heart is overflowing with a good theme; I recite my composition concerning the King; my tongue is the pen of a ready writer. ...Your throne, O God, is forever and ever; a scepter of righteousness is the scepter of Your kingdom."*

Psalm 47:2-3—*"For the Lord Most High is awesome; he is a great King over all the earth. He will subdue the peoples under us, and the nations under our feet."*

Psalm 72:7-8—*"In His days the righteous shall flourish, and abundance of peace, until the moon is no more. He shall have dominion also from sea to sea, and from the River to the ends of the earth."*

Psalm 74:12—*"For God is my King from of old, working salvation in the midst of the earth."*

Psalm 89:3-4—*"I have made a covenant with My chosen, I have sworn to My servant David: 'Your seed I will establish forever, and build up your throne to all generations.'"*

Psalm 89:27-35—*"Also I will make him My firstborn, the highest of the kings of the earth. My mercy I will keep for him forever, and My covenant shall stand firm with him. His seed also I will make to endure forever, and his throne as the days of Heaven. If his sons forsake My law and do not walk in My judgments, if they break My statutes and do not keep My commandments, then I will punish their transgression with the rod, and their iniquity with stripes. Nevertheless My lovingkindness I will not utterly take from him, nor allow My faithfulness to fail. My covenant I will not break, nor alter the word that has gone out of My lips. Once I have sworn by My holiness; I will not lie to David."*

Psalm 95:3—*"For the Lord is the great God, and the great King above all gods."*

Psalm 103:19—*"The Lord has established His throne in Heaven, and His kingdom rules over all."*

Psalm 115:16—*"The Heaven, even the heavens, are the Lord's; but the earth He has given to the children of men."*

Psalm 132:11-12—*"The Lord has sworn in truth to David; he will not turn from it: 'I will set upon your throne the fruit of your body. If your sons will keep My covenant and My testimony which I shall teach them, their sons also shall sit upon your throne forevermore.'"*

Psalm 145:10-13—*"All Your works shall praise You, O Lord, and Your saints shall bless You. They shall speak of the glory of Your kingdom, and talk of Your power, to make known to the sons of men His mighty acts, and the glorious majesty of His kingdom. Your kingdom is an everlasting kingdom, and Your dominion endures throughout all generations."*

Proverbs 19:12—*"The king's wrath is like the roaring of a lion, but his favor is like dew on the grass."*

Proverbs 20:2—*"The wrath of a king is like the roaring of a lion; whoever provokes him to anger sins against his own life."*

Proverbs 20:8—*"A king who sits on the throne of judgment scatters all evil with his eyes."*

Proverbs 20:26—*"A wise king sifts out the wicked, and brings the threshing wheel over them."*

Proverbs 20:28—*"Mercy and truth preserve the king, and by lovingkindness he upholds his throne."*

Proverbs 22:11—*"He who loves purity of heart and has grace on his lips, the king will be his friend."*

Proverbs 24:21—*"My son, fear the Lord and the king; do not associate with those given to change."*

Proverbs 25:5—*"Take away the wicked from before the king, and his throne will be established in righteousness."*

Proverbs 25:6—*"Do not exalt yourself in the presence of the king, and do not stand in the place of the great."*

Proverbs 29:4—*"The king establishes the land by justice, but he who receives bribes overthrows it."*

Proverbs 29:14—*"The king who judges the poor with truth, his throne will be established forever."*

Proverbs 30:31—"A greyhound, a male goat also, and a king whose troops are with him."

Isaiah 9:7—"Of the increase of His government and peace there will be no end, upon the throne of David and over His kingdom, to order it and establish it with judgment and justice from that time forward, even forever. The zeal of the Lord of hosts will perform this."

Isaiah 11:1-12—"There shall come forth a Rod from the stem of Jesse, and a Branch shall grow out of his roots. The Spirit of the Lord shall rest upon Him, the Spirit of wisdom and understanding, the Spirit of counsel and might, the Spirit of knowledge and of the fear of the Lord. His delight is in the fear of the Lord, and He shall not judge by the sight of His eyes, nor decide by the hearing of His ears; but with righteousness He shall judge the poor, and decide with equity for the meek of the earth; he shall strike the earth with the rod of His mouth, and with the breath of His lips He shall slay the wicked. Righteousness shall be the belt of His loins, and faithfulness the belt of His waist. The wolf also shall dwell with the lamb, the leopard shall lie down with the young goat, the calf and the young lion and the fatling together; and a little child shall lead them. The cow and the bear shall graze; their young ones shall lie down together; and the lion shall eat straw like the ox. The nursing child shall play by the cobra's hole, and the weaned child shall put his hand in the viper's den. They shall not hurt nor destroy in all My holy mountain, for the earth shall be full of the knowledge of the Lord as the waters cover the sea. And in that day there shall be a Root of Jesse, who shall stand as a banner to the people; for the Gentiles shall seek Him, and His resting place shall be glorious. It shall come to pass in that day that the Lord shall set His hand again the second time to recover the remnant of His people who are left, from Assyria and Egypt, from Pathros and Cush, from Elam and Shinar, from Hamath and the islands of the sea. He will set up a banner for the nations, and will assemble the outcasts of Israel, and gather together the dispersed of Judah from the four corners of the earth."

Jeremiah 23:5—"'Behold, the days are coming,' says the Lord, 'That I will raise to David a Branch of righteousness; a King shall reign and prosper, and execute judgment and righteousness in the earth.'"

Jeremiah 33:15-26— "In those days and at that time I will cause to grow up to David a Branch of righteousness; He shall execute judgment and righteousness in the earth. In those days Judah will be saved, and Jerusalem will dwell safely. And this is the name by which she will be called: 'the Lord our righteousness.' For thus says the Lord: 'David shall never lack a man to sit on the throne of the house of Israel; nor shall the priests, the Levites, lack a man to offer burnt offerings before Me, to kindle grain offerings, and to sacrifice continually.' And the word of the Lord came to Jeremiah, saying, 'Thus says the Lord: "If you can break My covenant with the day and My covenant with the night, so that there will not be day and night in their season, then My covenant may also be broken with David My servant, so that he shall not have a son to reign on his throne, and with the Levites, the priests, My minis-ters. As the host of Heaven cannot be numbered, nor the sand of the sea measured, so will I multiply the descendants of David My servant and the Levites who minister to Me."' Moreover the word of the Lord came to Jeremiah, saying, 'Have you not considered what these people have spoken, saying, "The two families which the Lord has chosen, He has also cast them off"? Thus they have despised My people, as if they should no more be a nation before them. Thus says the Lord: "If My covenant is not with day and night, and if I have not appointed the ordinances of Heaven and earth, then I will cast away the descendants of Jacob and David My servant, so that I will not take any of his descendants to be rulers over the descendants of Abraham, Isaac, and Jacob. For I will cause their captives to return, and will have mercy on them."'"

Daniel 2:44-45—"And in the days of these kings the God of Heaven will set up a kingdom which shall never be destroyed; and the kingdom shall not be left to other people; it shall break in pieces and consume all these kingdoms, and it shall stand forever. Inasmuch as you saw that the stone was cut out of the mountain without hands, and that it broke in pieces the iron, the bronze, the clay, the silver, and the gold—the great God has made known to the king what will come to pass after this. The dream is certain, and its interpretation is sure."

Daniel 4:3—"How great are His signs, and how mighty His wonders! His kingdom is an everlasting kingdom, and His dominion is from generation to generation."

Daniel 4:17—"This decision is by the decree of the watchers, and the sentence by the word of the holy ones, in order that the living may know that the Most High rules in the kingdom of men, gives it to whomever He will, and sets over it the lowest of men."

Daniel 6:26—"I make a decree that in every dominion of my kingdom men must tremble and fear before the God of Daniel. For He is the living God, and steadfast forever; his kingdom is the one which shall not be destroyed, and His dominion shall endure to the end."

Daniel 7:14—"Then to Him was given dominion and glory and a kingdom, that all peoples, nations, and languages should serve

Him. His dominion is an everlasting dominion, which shall not pass away, and His kingdom the one which shall not be destroyed."

Daniel 7:18—*"But the saints of the Most High shall receive the kingdom, and possess the kingdom forever, even forever and ever."*

Daniel 7:22—*"Until the Ancient of Days came, and a judgment was made in favor of the saints of the Most High, and the time came for the saints to possess the kingdom."*

Daniel 7:27—*"Then the Kingdom and dominion, and the greatness of the kingdoms under the whole Heaven, shall be given to the people, the saints of the Most High. His kingdom is an everlasting kingdom, and all dominions shall serve and obey Him."*

Obadiah 1:21—*"Then saviors shall come to Mount Zion to judge the mountains of Esau, and the kingdom shall be the Lord's."*

Zechariah 9:9-10—*"Rejoice greatly, O daughter of Zion! Shout, O daughter of Jerusalem! Behold, your King is coming to you; he is just and having salvation, lowly and riding on a donkey, a colt, the foal of a donkey. I will cut off the chariot from Ephraim and the horse from Jerusalem; the battle bow shall be cut off. He shall speak peace to the nations; his dominion shall be 'from sea to sea, and from the River to the ends of the earth.'"*

New Testament

Matthew 3:1-2—*"In those days John the Baptist came preaching in the wilderness of Judea, and saying, "Repent, for the kingdom of Heaven is at hand!"*

Matthew 4:17—*"From that time Jesus began to preach and to say, 'Repent, for the kingdom of Heaven is at hand.'"*

Matthew 4:23—*"And Jesus went about all Galilee, teaching in their synagogues, preaching the gospel of the kingdom, and healing all kinds of sickness and all kinds of disease among the people."*

Matthew 5:3—*"Blessed are the poor in spirit, for theirs is the kingdom of Heaven."*

Matthew 5:10—*"Blessed are those who are persecuted for righteousness' sake, for theirs is the kingdom of Heaven."*

Matthew 5:19—*"Whoever therefore breaks one of the least of these commandments, and teaches men so, shall be called least in the kingdom of Heaven; but whoever does and teaches them, he shall be called great in the kingdom of Heaven."*

Matthew 5:20—*"For I say to you, that unless your righteousness exceeds the righteousness of the scribes and Pharisees, you will by no means enter the kingdom of Heaven."*

Matthew 6:10—*"Your kingdom come. Your will be done on earth as it is in Heaven."*

Matthew 6:33—*"But seek first the kingdom of God and His righteousness, and all these things shall be added to you."*

Matthew 7:21—*"Not everyone who says to Me, 'Lord, Lord,' shall enter the kingdom of Heaven, but he who does the will of My Father in Heaven."*

Matthew 9:35—*"Then Jesus went about all the cities and villages, teaching in their synagogues, preaching the gospel of the kingdom, and healing every sickness and every disease among the people."*

Matthew 10:7-8—*"And as you go, preach, saying, 'The kingdom of Heaven is at hand.' Heal the sick, cleanse the lepers, raise the dead, cast out demons. Freely you have received, freely give."*

Matthew 11:11-12—*"Assuredly, I say to you, among those born of women there has not risen one greater than John the Baptist; but he who is least in the kingdom of Heaven is greater than he. And from the days of John the Baptist until now the kingdom of Heaven suffers violence, and the violent take it by force."*

Matthew 12:25-28—*"But Jesus knew their thoughts, and said to them: 'Every kingdom divided against itself is brought to desolation, and every city or house divided against itself will not stand. If Satan casts out Satan, he is divided against himself. How then will his kingdom stand? And if I cast out demons by Beelzebub, by whom do your sons cast them out? Therefore they shall be your judges. But if I cast out demons by the Spirit of God, surely the kingdom of God has come upon you.'"*

Matthew 13:11—*"He answered and said to them, 'Because it has been given to you to know the mysteries of the kingdom of Heaven, but to them it has not been given.'"*

Matthew 13:19—*"When anyone hears the word of the kingdom, and does not understand it, then the wicked one comes and snatches away what was sown in his heart. This is he who received seed by the wayside."*

Matthew 13:24-33—*"Another parable He put forth to them, saying: 'The Kingdom of Heaven is like a man who sowed good seed in his field; but while men slept, his enemy came and sowed tares among the wheat and went his way. But when the grain had sprouted and produced a crop, then the tares also appeared. So the servants of the owner came and said to him, "Sir, did you not sow good seed in your field? How then does it have tares?" He said to them, "An enemy has done this." The servants said to him, "Do you want us then to go and gather them up?" But he said, "No, lest while you gather up the tares you also uproot the wheat with them. Let both grow together until the harvest, and at the time of harvest I will say to the reapers, 'First gather together the tares and bind them in bundles to burn them, but gather the wheat into my barn.'" Another parable He put forth to them, saying: 'The kingdom of Heaven is like a mustard seed, which a man took and sowed in his field, which indeed is the least of all the seeds; but when it is grown it is greater than the herbs and becomes a tree, so that the birds of the air come and nest in its branches.' Another parable He spoke to them: 'The kingdom of Heaven is like leaven, which a woman took and hid in three measures of meal till it was all leavened.'"*

Matthew 13:38-52—*"'The field is the world, the good seeds are the sons of the kingdom, but the tares are the sons of the wicked one. The enemy who sowed them is the devil, the harvest is the end of the age, and the reapers are the angels. Therefore as the tares are gathered and burned in the fire, so it will be at the end of this age. The Son of Man will send out His angels, and they will gather out of His kingdom all things that offend, and those who practice lawlessness, and will cast them into the furnace of fire. There will be wailing and gnashing of teeth. Then the righteous will shine forth as the sun in the kingdom of their Father. He who has ears to hear, let him hear! Again, the kingdom of Heaven is like treasure hidden in a field, which a man found and hid; and for joy over it he goes and sells all that he has and buys that field. Again, the kingdom of Heaven is like a merchant seeking beautiful pearls, who, when he had found one pearl of great price, went and sold all that he had and bought it. Again, the kingdom of Heaven is like a dragnet that was cast into the sea and gathered some of every kind, which, when it was full, they drew to shore; and they sat down and gathered the good into vessels, but threw the bad away. So it will be at the end of the age. The angels will come forth, separate the wicked from among the just, and cast them into the furnace of fire. There will be wailing and gnashing of teeth.' Jesus said to them, 'Have you understood all these things?' They said to Him, 'Yes, Lord.' Then He said to them, 'Therefore every scribe instructed concerning the kingdom of Heaven is like a householder who brings out of his treasure things new and old.'"*

Matthew 16:19—*"And I will give you the keys of the kingdom of Heaven, and whatever you bind on earth will be bound in Heaven, and whatever you loose on earth will be loosed in Heaven."*

Matthew 16:28—*"Assuredly, I say to you, there are some standing here who shall not taste death till they see the Son of Man coming in His kingdom."*

Matthew 18:1-4—*"At that time the disciples came to Jesus, saying, 'Who then is greatest in the kingdom of heaven?' Then Jesus called a little child to Him, set him in the midst of them, and said, 'Assuredly, I say to you, unless you are converted and become as little children, you will by no means enter the kingdom of Heaven. Therefore whoever humbles himself as this little child is the greatest in the kingdom of Heaven.'"*

Matthew 18:23-35—*"Therefore the kingdom of Heaven is like a certain king who wanted to settle accounts with his servants. And when he had begun to settle accounts, one was brought to him who owed him ten thousand talents. But as he was not able to pay, his master commanded that he be sold, with his wife and children and all that he had, and that payment be made. The servant therefore fell down before him, saying, 'Master, have patience with me, and I will pay you all.' Then the master of that servant was moved with compassion, released him, and forgave him the debt. But that servant went out and found one of his fellow servants who owed him a hundred denarii; and he laid hands on him and took him by the throat, saying, 'Pay me what you owe!' So his fellow servant fell down at his feet and begged him, saying, 'Have patience with me, and I will pay you all.' And he would not, but went and threw him into prison till he should pay the debt. So when his fellow servants saw what had been done, they were very grieved, and came and told their master all that had been done. Then his master, after he had called him, said to him, 'You wicked servant! I forgave you all that debt because you begged me. Should you not also have had compassion on your fellow servant, just as I had pity on you?' And his master was angry, and delivered him to the torturers until he should pay all that was due to him. So My heavenly Father also will do to you if each of you, from his heart, does not forgive his brother his trespasses."*

Matthew 19:14—*"But Jesus said, 'Let the little children come to Me, and do not forbid them; for of such is the kingdom of Heaven.'"*

Matthew 19:24—*"And again I say to you, it is easier for a camel to go through the eye of a needle than for a rich man to enter the kingdom of God."*

Matthew 20:1-16—*"For the kingdom of Heaven is like a land-owner who went out early in the morning to hire laborers for his vineyard. Now when he had agreed with the laborers for a denarius a day, he sent them into his vineyard. And he went out about the third hour and saw others standing idle in the marketplace, and said to them, 'You also go into the vineyard, and whatever is right I will give you.' So they went. Again he went out about the sixth and the ninth hour, and did likewise. And about the eleventh hour he went out and found others standing idle, and said to them, 'Why have you been standing here idle all day?' They said to him, 'Because no one hired us.' He said to them, 'You also go into the vineyard, and whatever is right you will receive.' So when evening had come, the owner of the vineyard said to his steward, 'Call the laborers and give them their wages, beginning with the last to the first.' And when those came who were hired about the eleventh hour, they each received a denarius.*

But when the first came, they supposed that they would receive more; and they likewise received each a denarius. And when they had received it, they complained against the landowner, saying, 'These last men have worked only one hour, and you made them equal to us who have borne the burden and the heat of the day.' But he answered one of them and said, 'Friend, I am doing you no wrong. Did you not agree with me for a denarius? Take what is yours and go your way. I wish to give to this last man the same as to you. Is it not lawful for me to do what I wish with my own things? Or is your eye evil because I am good?' So the last will be first, and the first last. For many are called, but few chosen."

Matthew 21:28-32—*"But what do you think? A man had two sons, and he came to the first and said, "Son, go, work today in my vineyard." He answered and said, "I will not," but afterward he regretted it and went. Then he came to the second and said likewise. And he answered and said, "I go, sir," but he did not go. Which of the two did the will of his father?' They said to Him, 'The first.' Jesus said to them, 'Assuredly, I say to you that tax collectors and harlots enter the kingdom of God before you. For John came to you in the way of righteousness, and you did not believe him; but tax collectors and harlots believed him; and when you saw it, you did not afterward relent and believe him.'"*

Matthew 22:2-14—*"The kingdom of Heaven is like a certain king who arranged a marriage for his son, and sent out his servants to call those who were invited to the wedding; and they were not willing to come. Again, he sent out other servants, saying, 'Tell those who are invited, "See, I have prepared my dinner; my oxen and fatted cattle are killed, and all things are ready. Come to the wedding."' But they made light of it and went their ways, one to his own farm, another to his business. And the rest seized his servants, treated them spitefully, and killed them. But when the king heard about it, he was furious. And he sent out his armies, destroyed those murderers, and burned up their city. Then he said to his servants, 'The wedding is ready, but those who were invited were not worthy. Therefore go into the highways, and as many as you find, invite to the wedding.' So those servants went out into the highways and gathered together all whom they found, both bad and good. And the wedding hall was filled with guests. But when the king came in to see the guests, he saw a man there who did not have on a wedding garment. So he said to him, 'Friend, how did you come in here without a wedding garment?' And he was speechless. Then the king said to the servants, 'Bind him hand and foot, take him away, and cast him into outer darkness; there will be weeping and gnashing of teeth.' For many are called, but few are chosen."*

Matthew 21:43—*"Therefore I say to you, the kingdom of God will be taken from you and given to a nation bearing the fruits of it."*

Matthew 23:13—*"But woe to you, scribes and Pharisees, hypocrites! For you shut up the kingdom of Heaven against men; for you neither go in yourselves, nor do you allow those who are entering to go in."*

Matthew 24:14—*"And this gospel of the kingdom will be preached in all the world as a witness to all the nations, and then the end will come."*

Matthew 25:1,13-36—*"Then the kingdom of Heaven shall be likened to ten virgins who took their lamps and went out to meet the bridegroom. ...Watch therefore, for you know neither the day nor the hour in which the Son of Man is coming. For the kingdom of Heaven is like a man traveling to a far country, who called his own servants and delivered his goods to them. And to one he gave five talents, to another two, and to another one, to each according to his own ability; and immediately he went on a journey. Then he who had received the five talents went and traded with them, and made another five talents. And likewise he who had received two gained two more also. But he who had received one went and dug in the ground, and hid his lord's money. After a long time the lord of those servants came and settled accounts with them. So he who had received five talents came and brought five other talents, saying, 'Lord, you delivered to me five talents; look, I have gained five more talents besides them.' His lord said to him, 'Well done, good and faithful servant; you were faithful over a few things, I will make you ruler over many things. Enter into the joy of your lord.' He also who had received two talents came and said, 'Lord, you delivered to me two talents; look, I have gained two more talents besides them.' His lord said to him, 'Well done, good and faithful servant; you have been faithful over a few things, I will make you ruler over many things. Enter into the joy of your lord.' Then he who had received the one talent came and said, 'Lord, I knew you to be a hard man, reaping where you have not sown, and gathering where you have not scattered seed. And I was afraid, and went and hid your talent in the ground. Look, there you have what is yours.' But his lord answered and said to him, 'You wicked and lazy servant, you knew that I reap where I have not sown, and gather where I have not scattered seed. So you ought to have deposited my money with the bankers, and at my coming I would have received back my own with interest. So take the talent from him, and give it to him who has ten talents. For to everyone who has, more will be given, and he will have abundance; but from him who does not have, even what he has will be taken away. And cast the unprofitable servant into the outer darkness. There will be weeping and gnashing of teeth.' When the Son of Man comes in His glory, and all the holy angels with Him, then He will sit on the throne of His glory. All the nations will be gathered before Him, and He will separate them one from another, as a shepherd divides his sheep from the goats. And He will set the sheep on His right hand, but the goats on the left. Then the King will say to those on His right hand, 'Come, you blessed of My Father, inherit the Kingdom prepared for you from the foundation of the world: for I was hungry and you gave Me food; I was thirsty and you gave Me drink; I was a stranger and you took Me in; I was naked and you clothed Me; I was sick and you visited Me; I was in prison and you came to Me.'"*

Matthew 26:29—*"But I say to you, I will not drink of this fruit of the vine from now on until that day when I drink it new with you in My Father's kingdom."*

Mark 1:14-15—*"Now after John was put in prison, Jesus came to Galilee, preaching the gospel of the kingdom of God, and saying, 'The time is fulfilled, and the kingdom of God is at hand. Repent, and believe in the gospel.'"*

Mark 4:26-32—*"And He said, 'The kingdom of God is as if a man should scatter seed on the ground, and should sleep by night and rise by day, and the seed should sprout and grow, he himself does not know how. For the earth yields crops by itself: first the blade, then the head, after that the full grain in the head. But when the grain ripens, immediately he puts in the sickle, because the harvest has come.' Then He said, 'To what shall we liken the king-dom of God? Or with what parable shall we picture it? It is like a mustard seed which, when it is sown on the ground, is smaller than all the seeds on earth; but when it is sown, it grows up and becomes greater than all herbs, and shoots out large branches, so that the birds of the air may nest under its shade.'"*

Mark 9:47-48—*"And if your eye causes you to sin, pluck it out. It is better for you to enter the kingdom of God with one eye, rather than having two eyes, to be cast into hell fire—where 'their worm does not die, and the fire is not quenched.'"*

Mark 11:9-10—*"Then those who went before and those who fol-lowed cried out, saying: 'Hosanna! Blessed is He who comes in the name of the Lord! Blessed is the kingdom of our father David that comes in the name of the Lord! Hosanna in the highest!'"*

Mark 12:28-34—*"Then one of the scribes came, and having heard them reasoning together, perceiving that He had answered them well, asked Him, 'Which is the first commandment of all?' Jesus answered him, 'The first of all the commandments is: "Hear, O Israel, the Lord our God, the Lord is one. And you shall love the Lord your God with all your heart, with all your soul, with all your mind, and with all your strength." This is the first command-ment. And the second, like it, is this: "You shall love your neighbor as yourself." There is no other commandment greater than these.' So the scribe said to Him, 'Well said, Teacher. You have spoken the truth, for there is one God, and there is no other but He. And to love Him with all the heart, with all the understanding, with all the soul, and with all the strength, and to love one's neighbor as oneself, is more than all the whole burnt offerings and sacrifices.' Now when Jesus saw that he answered wisely, He said to him, 'You are not far from the kingdom of God.' But after that no one dared question Him."*

Luke 1:30-33—*"Then the angel said to her, 'Do not be afraid, Mary, for you have found favor with God. And behold, you will conceive in your womb and bring forth a Son, and shall call His name Jesus. He will be great, and will be called the Son of the Highest; and the Lord God will give Him the throne of His father David. And He will reign over the house of Jacob forever, and of His kingdom there will be no end.'"*

Luke 4:43—*"But He said to them, 'I must preach the kingdom of God to the other cities also, because for this purpose I have been sent.'"*

Luke 8:1—*"Now it came to pass, afterward, that He went through every city and village, preaching and bringing the glad tidings of the kingdom of God. And the twelve were with Him."*

Luke 9:60-62—*"Jesus said to him, 'Let the dead bury their own dead, but you go and preach the kingdom of God.' And another also said, 'Lord, I will follow You, but let me first go and bid them farewell who are at my house.' But Jesus said to him, 'No one, having put his hand to the plow, and looking back, is fit for the kingdom of God.'"*

Luke 10:9—*"And heal the sick there, and say to them, 'The kingdom of God has come near to you.'"*

Luke 11:20—*"But if I cast out demons with the finger of God, surely the kingdom of God has come upon you."*

Luke 12:29-31—*"And do not seek what you should eat or what you should drink, nor have an anxious mind. For all these things the nations of the world seek after, and your Father knows that you need these things. But seek the kingdom of God, and all these things shall be added to you."*

Luke 12:32—*"Do not fear, little flock, for it is your Father's good pleasure to give you the kingdom."*

Luke 13:28-29—*"There will be weeping and gnashing of teeth, when you see Abraham and Isaac and Jacob and all the prophets in the kingdom of God, and yourselves thrust out. They will come from the east and the west, from the north and the south, and sit down in the kingdom of God."*

Luke 16:15-16—*"And He said to them, 'You are those who justify yourselves before men, but God knows your hearts. For what is highly esteemed among men is an abomination in the sight of God. The law and the prophets were until John. Since that time the kingdom of God has been preached, and everyone is pressing into it.'"*

Luke 17:20-21—*"Now when He was asked by the Pharisees when the kingdom of God would come, He answered them and said, 'The kingdom of God does not come with observation; nor will they say, "See here!" or "See there!" For indeed, the kingdom of God is within you.'"*

Luke 18:29-30—*"So He said to them, 'Assuredly, I say to you, there is no one who has left house or parents or brothers or wife or children, for the sake of the kingdom of God, who shall not receive many times more in this present time, and in the age to come everlasting life.'"*

Luke 19:11-27—*"Now as they heard these things, He spoke another parable, because He was near Jerusalem and because they thought the kingdom of God would appear immediately. Therefore He said: 'A certain nobleman went into a far country* to receive for himself a kingdom and to return. So he called ten of his servants, delivered to them ten minas, and said to them, "Do business till I come." But his citizens hated him, and sent a delegation after him, saying, "We will not have this man to reign over us." And so it was that when he returned, having received the kingdom, he then commanded these servants, to whom he had given the money, to be called to him, that he might know how much every man had gained by trading. Then came the first, saying, "Master, your mina has earned ten minas." And he said to him, "Well done, good servant; because you were faithful in a very little, have authority over ten cities." And the second came, saying, "Master, your mina has earned five minas." Likewise he said to him, "You also be over five cities." Then another came, saying, "Master, here is your mina, which I have kept put away in a handkerchief. For I feared you, because you are an austere man. You collect what you did not deposit, and reap what you did not sow." And he said to him, "Out of your own mouth I will judge you, you wicked servant. You knew that I was an austere man, collecting what I did not deposit and reaping what I did not sow. Why then did you not put my money in the bank, that at my coming I might have collected it with interest?" And he said to those who stood by, "Take the mina from him, and give it to him who has ten minas." (But they said to him, "Master, he has ten minas.") "For I say to you, that to everyone who has will be given; and from him who does not have, even what he has will be taken away from him. But bring here those enemies of mine, who did not want me to reign over them, and slay them before me.""

Luke 21:31—"So you also, when you see these things happening, know that the Kingdom of God is near."

Luke 22:29-30—*"And I bestow upon you a kingdom, just as My Father bestowed one upon Me, that you may eat and drink at My table in My kingdom, and sit on thrones judging the twelve tribes of Israel."*

Luke 23:42-43—*"Then he said to Jesus, 'Lord, remember me when You come into Your kingdom.' And Jesus said to him, 'Assuredly, I say to you, today you will be with Me in Paradise.'"*

John 3:3-5—*"Jesus answered and said to him, 'Most assuredly, I say to you, unless one is born again, he cannot see the Kingdom of God.' Nicodemus said to Him, 'How can a man be born when he is old? Can he enter a second time into his mother's womb and be born?' Jesus answered, 'Most assuredly, I say to you, unless one is born of water and the Spirit, he cannot enter the Kingdom of God.'"*

John 18:36—*"Jesus answered, 'My kingdom is not of this world. If My kingdom were of this world, My servants would fight, so that I should not be delivered to the Jews; but now My kingdom is not from here.'"*

Acts 1:3—*"To whom He also presented Himself alive after His suffering by many infallible proofs, being seen by them during forty days and speaking of the things pertaining to the kingdom of God."*

Acts 8:12—*"But when they believed Philip as he preached the things concerning the kingdom of God and the name of Jesus Christ, both men and women were baptized."*

Acts 14:22—*"Strengthening the souls of the disciples, exhorting them to continue in the faith, and saying, 'We must through many tribulations enter the Kingdom of God.'"*

Acts 19:8—*"And he went into the synagogue and spoke boldly for three months, reasoning and persuading concerning the things of the kingdom of God."*

Acts 20:25—*"And indeed, now I know that you all, among whom I have gone preaching the kingdom of God, will see my face no more."*

Acts 28:23—*"So when they had appointed him a day, many came to him at his lodging, to whom he explained and solemnly testified of the kingdom of God, persuading them concerning Jesus from both the Law of Moses and the Prophets, from morning till evening."*

Acts 28:30-31—*"Then Paul dwelt two whole years in his own rented house, and received all who came to him, preaching the kingdom of God and teaching the things which concern the Lord Jesus Christ with all confidence, no one forbidding him."*

Romans 14:17—*"For the kingdom of God is not eating and drinking, but righteousness and peace and joy in the Holy Spirit."*

1 Corinthians 4:20—*"For the kingdom of God is not in word but in power."*

1 Corinthians 6:9-11—*"Do you not know that the unrighteous will not inherit the kingdom of God? Do not be deceived. Neither fornicators, nor idolaters, nor adulterers, nor homosexuals, nor sodomites, nor thieves, nor covetous, nor drunkards, nor revilers, nor extortioners will inherit the kingdom of God. And such were some of you. But you were washed, but you were sanctified, but you were justified in the name of the Lord Jesus and by the Spirit of our God."*

1 Corinthians 15:22-26—*"For as in Adam all die, even so in Christ all shall be made alive. But each one in his own order: Christ the*

firstfruits, afterward those who are Christ's at His coming. Then comes the end, when He delivers the kingdom to God the Father, when He puts an end to all rule and all authority and power. For He must reign till He has put all enemies under His feet. The last enemy that will be destroyed is death."

1 Corinthians 15:50—*"Now this I say, brethren, that flesh and blood cannot inherit the kingdom of God; nor does corruption inherit incorruption."*

Galatians 5:19-21—*"Now the works of the flesh are evident, which are: adultery, fornication, uncleanness, lewdness, idolatry, sorcery, hatred, contentions, jealousies, outbursts of wrath, selfish ambitions, dissensions, heresies, envy, murders, drunkenness, revelries, and the like; of which I tell you beforehand, just as I also told you in time past, that those who practice such things will not inherit the kingdom of God."*

Ephesians 5:5—*"For this you know, that no fornicator, unclean person, nor covetous man, who is an idolater, has any inheritance in the kingdom of Christ and God."*

Colossians 1:13—*"He has delivered us from the power of darkness and conveyed us into the kingdom of the Son of His love."*

Hebrews 12:28—*"Therefore, since we are receiving a kingdom which cannot be shaken, let us have grace, by which we may serve God acceptably with reverence and godly fear."*

James 2:5—*"Listen, my beloved brethren: has God not chosen the poor of this world to be rich in faith and heirs of the kingdom which He promised to those who love Him?"*

1 Peter 2:17—*"Fear God. Honor the King."*

Jude 1:14-15—*"Now Enoch, the seventh from Adam, prophesied about these men also, saying, 'Behold, the Lord comes with ten thousands of His saints, to execute judgment on all, to convict all who are ungodly among them of all their ungodly deeds which they have committed in an ungodly way, and of all the harsh things which ungodly sinners have spoken against Him.'"*

Revelation 11:15—*"The kingdoms of this world have become the kingdoms of our Lord and of His Christ, and He shall reign forever and ever!"*

Revelation 12:10—*"Then I heard a loud voice saying in Heaven, 'Now salvation, and strength, and the kingdom of our God, and the power of His Christ have come, for the accuser of our brethren, who accused them before our God day and night, has been cast down.'"*

Bibliography

Baker, H.A. *Visions Beyond The Veil*. Public Domain.

Barnes, Albert. *Barnes' Notes*. Computer software. Seattle, WA: Biblesoft, 1997.

Brown, Francis, S. Driver, and C. Briggs. *Brown, Driver and Briggs' Hebrew Lexicon*. Ontario, Canada: Woodside Bible Fellowship, 1993.

Clarke, Adam. *Clarke's Commentary*. Computer software. Seattle, WA: Biblesoft, 1996.

Conner, Kevin J. *Interpreting the Symbols and Types*. Portland, OR: City Bible Publishing, 1980.

Comfort, Ray, *How to Win Souls and Influence People*. New Brunswick, NJ: Bridge-Logos Publishers, 1999.

Dake, Finis J. *Dake's Annotated Reference Bible*. Lawrencevill, GA: Dake Bible Sales, Inc., 1963.

Dummelow, J.R. *A One Volume Bible Commentary*. New York, NY: Macmillan Company, 1908.

Eldredge, John. *Waking the Dead*. Nashville, TN: Thomas Nelson, 2003.

Fletcher, Kingsley. *I Have Seen the Kingdom*. Orlando, FL: Creation House, 1998.

Hansel, Tim. *Holy Sweat*. Dallas, TX: Word, 1987.

Henrey, Matthew. *Matthew Henry Commentary on the Whole Bible*. Peabody, MA: Hendrickson, Inc., 1991.

Jamison, Fausset and Brown Commentary. Computer software. Seattle, WA: Biblesoft, 1997.

Johnson, Bill. *The Supernatural Power of a Transformed Mind*. Shippensburg, PA: Destiny Image, 2005.

Johnson, Bill. *When Heaven Invades Earth*. Shippensburg, PA: Destiny Image, 2003.

Joyner, Rick. "Taking the Land, Seeking the Kingdom." *Elijahlist.com* (2006).

Keil, C.F., and F. Delitzsch. *Keil and Delitzsch Commentary on the Old Testament*. Vol. 1. Grand Rapids, MI: Eerdman's Company, 1980.

Ladd, George E. *The Gospel of the Kingdom*. Grand Rapids, MI: Eerdman's Company, 1959.

Lairdon, Roberts. *God's Generals*. Tulsa, OK: Albury, 1996.

Lake, John G. *Adventures in God*. Tulsa, OK: Harrison House, 1981.

Lake, John G., and Kenneth Copeland. *John G. Lake: His Life, His Sermons, His Boldness of Faith*. Fort Worth, TX: Kenneth Copeland Publications, 1994.

Lancaster, D. Thomas. *The Mystery Of The Gospel*. Littleton, CO: First Fruits Of Zion, 2003.

Larson, Craig B. *Illustrations for Preaching and Teaching*. Grand Rapids, MI: Baker Books, 1993.

Lindsay, Gordon. *John G. Lake Sermons on Dominion, over Demons, Disease and Death*. Dallas, TX: Christ for the Nations, Inc., 1949.

Mason, John. *Know Your Limitations, Then Ignore Them*. Tulsa, OK: Insight Publishing Group, 1999

Mays, James L. *Harper's Bible Commentary*. New York, NY: HarperCollins, 1988.

Monroe, Myles. *Kingdom Principles*. Shippensburg, PA: Destiny Image, 2006.

Monroe, Myles. *Rediscovering the Kingdom*. Shippensburg, PA: Destiny Image, 2004.

Nee, Watchman. *Let Us Pray*. New York, NY: Christian Fellowship, Inc., 1978.

Nee, Watchman. *Not I but Christ*. New York, NY: Christian Fellowship, Inc., 1974.

Nee, Watchman. *The Communion of the Holy Spirit*. New York, NY: Christian Fellowship, Inc., 1994.

Nee, Watchman. *The King and the Kingdom*. New York, NY: Christian Fellowship, Inc., 1978.

Nee, Watchman. *The Spirit of Wisdom and Revelation*. New York, NY: Christian Fellowship, Inc., 1980.

Nelson's Illustrated Bible Dictionary. Nashville: Thomas Nelson, 1986.

New Bible Dictionary. Downers Grove, IL: Intervarsity Press, 1962.

Orr, James. *International Standard Bible Encyclopedia*. Computer software. 1915 Edition. Seattle, WA: Biblesoft, 1995–1996.

Peterson, Eugene. *The Message*. Colorado Springs, CO: NavPress Group, 1993.

Pfeiffer, Charles E., and Everett F. Harrison. The Wycliffe Bible Commentary. Chicago, IL: Moody Press, 1962.

Pratney, Winkie. *Revival*. Springdale, PA: Whitaker House, 1983.

Reidt, Wilford. *John G. Lake: A Man Without Compromise*. Tulsa, OK: Harrison House, 1989.

Robertson, Pat. *The Secret Kingdom*. Nashville, TN: Thomas Nelson, 1982.

Smith, Sean. *Prophetic Evangelism*. Shippensburg, PA: Destiny Image, 2004.

Steele, Ron *Plundering Hell to Populate Heaven*. Laguna Hills, CA: Reinhard Bonnke Ministries, 1987

Stern, David H. *Jewish New Testament Commentary*. Clarksville, MD: Jewish New Testament Publications, Inc., 1992.

Strong, James. *New Exhaustive Strong's Numbers and Concordance with Expanded Greek-Hebrew Dictionary*. Nashville, TN: Thomas Nelson Inc., 1994.

Tenney, Merrill C. *The Zondervan Pictorial Encyclopedia of the Bible*. Grand Rapids, MI: Zondervan House, 1975.

Thayer, Joseph. *Thayer's Greek Lexicon*. Ontario, Canada: Woodside Bible Fellowship, 1993.

Tozer, A.W. *The Knowledge of the Holy*. New York, NY: Harper and Brothers, 1961.

Tozer, A.W. *The Pursuit of God*. Wheaton, IL: Tyndale House, 1982.

Unger, Merrill F. *The New Unger's Bible Dictionary*. Chicago, IL: Moody Press, 1985.

Warren, Rick. *The Purpose-Driven Life*. Grand Rapids, MI: Zondervan House, 2002.

Zodhiates, Spiros. *The Complete Wordstudy New Testament*. Chattanooga, TN: AMG Publishers, 1992.

Zuck, Roy B. *The Speaker's Quote Book*. Grand Rapids, MI: Kregel Publications, 1997.

Let It Go!:
Letting forgiveness lead you to a liberated heart. 2-CD Series

Staying Up in a Down World:
The transforming power of encouragement. 2-CD Series

Keep It Real:
Reality Christianity. 2-CD Series

New Born Identity:
Remember who you are. 2-CD Series

Revolutionaries:
History belongs to those who don't. 2-CD Series

Spiritual Body Piercing:
In the end all will be marked. 2-CD Series

To place an order, visit HtmlResAnchor www.SQInt.org

For booking, contact:

SoleQuest International, www.SQInt.org

Office Phone: 925-963-4665

Additional copies of this book and other
book titles from Destiny Image are
available at your local bookstore.

Call toll-free: 1-800-722-6774.

Send a request for a catalog to:

Destiny Image® Publishers, Inc.
P.O. Box 310
Shippensburg, PA 17257-0310

*"Speaking to the Purposes of God for This
Generation and for the Generations to Come."*

**For a complete list of our titles,
visit us at www.destinyimage.com.**